MEMORIES OF A COUNTRY BOY
1889 - 1902

Written by John Aloysius Miller

Compiled & Edited by
Christopher Locke, a Grandson

CenterLine Publishing
& Consulting LLC
CL

I dedicate this work to my Mother, without who's tender care during three serious illnesses I might not have lived to become a man.

John Aloysius Miller

CONTENTS

AUTHOR'S NOTE

This work was written for my grandchildren, to give them an insight into the modes of living on a farm in southern Indiana in the Gay Nineties.

The events related here are true and it is my hope the reader will accept them in the sincerity with which they were written.

If some of them seem somewhat out of the ordinary, please remember, most of them happened almost seventy years ago. *[Editor: Actually, 131 years ago as of 2020]*

The Author

EDITOR'S NOTE

My Grandfather, John Aloysius Miller, wrote this book in 1964. It was completed by August 16th, his 75th birthday. This book is an extremely detailed, candid, historical account of his life growing up on a farm in southwest Indiana, beginning with his birth in 1889 and ending in 1902 when he was 13 years old.

My Grandfather was a virtuous, God-fearing, talented man. And as you will soon find out, he had the memory of an elephant, even at the age of nearly 75 when he wrote this book. His upbringing and adolescent experiences were so notable that he never forgot a day of it, right down to names, dates, physical entities, and event narratives. These incredibly documented writings are not only a treasure for his descendants, but they offer America a firsthand glimpse into a world that no longer exists – a world with few eyewitness accounts available, at least not with this extraordinary detail.

Although the Müller house and farm described in this book have been gone for decades, the exact location where they once stood has been verified. The property is within the municipality limits of Wadesville, Indiana, just two-and-a-half miles east of downtown Wadesville, at the southwest intersection of Blake Road (running east and west) and Schmitt Road (running north and south, starting at Blake Road). By the way, Schmitt Road is named after my Grandfather's relatives on his mother's side whose descendants still farm, about a mile south of where the Müller property was located.

In order to provide a historical perspective on what was occurring in the world during the time-period this book was written about, the following are major world headlines between 1889 and 1902:

1889: The Eiffel Tower is inaugurated in Paris.
1889: The Johnstown Flood in Pennsylvania, killing 2,209 people.
1889: Vincent van Gogh paints Starry Night.
1889: Aspirin is patented.
1889: Moulin Rouge opens in Paris.
1890: The Wounded Knee Massacre in South Dakota.
1890: Death of Vincent van Gogh.
1890: The cardboard box is invented.
1891: Wrigley (gum) Company is founded in Illinois.
1892: Basketball is invented.

1892: The World's Columbian Exposition was held in Chicago celebrating the 400th anniversary of Christopher Columbus's arrival in the New World. Note that the Exposition is covered in this book.

1892: Tchaikovsky's Nutcracker Suite premières in Russia.

1892: John Froelich constructs the first gasoline-powered tractor.

1893: U.S. forces overthrow the government of Hawaii.

1894: First commercial film release by Jean Aimé Le Roy.

1894: First gramophone record.

1895: Volleyball is invented.

1895: Wilhelm Röntgen identifies x-rays.

1896: Olympic Games revived in Athens.

1896: Philippine Revolution ends declaring Philippines free from Spanish rule.

1896: Klondike Gold Rush in Canada.

1896: Henri Becquerel discovers radioactivity; J. J. Thomson identifies the electron, though not by name.

1897: Bram Stoker writes Dracula.

1897: First electric bicycle produced by Hosea Libbey.

1898: The USS Maine exploded in Havana harbor which leads to the Spanish-American War.

1898: H. G. Wells publishes The War of the Worlds

1898-1900: Zeppelin LZ 1 airship first produced.

1899–1902: Second Boer War begins.

1899–1913: Philippine–American War begins.

1899–1900: Indian famine kills over 1 million people.

1900: Hawaii becomes an official U.S. territory.

1900: Galveston Hurricane in Texas kills 8000 people.

1900: L. Frank Baum publishes The Wonderful Wizard of Oz.

1901: First Nobel Prizes awarded.

1901: Upon the death of Queen Victoria, Edward VII becomes King of the United Kingdom and the British Dominions

1901: Assassination of William McKinley.

1901: Guglielmo Marconi receives the first trans-Atlantic radio signal in St. John, Newfoundland.

1902: Philippine–American War ends.

1902: Cuba gains independence from the United States.

1902: Willis Carrier invents the world's first modern electrical air conditioning unit.

MEMORIES OF A COUNTRY BOY
1889 - 1902

CHAPTER ONE

I was born on Friday, August 16, 1889, on a farm located sixteen miles northwest of Evansville, Indiana, exactly one week after the death of my older brother. He was twenty-six months old when he died in my mother's arms of whooping cough.

I was a sickly child when I was born, as I had a hernia at birth. After two months of trusses and treatments had failed to correct the trouble, I was operated on at home by a professor from Cincinnati, Ohio. Because of my tender age, only a mild anesthetic was administered, and I was therefore only in a stupor during the entire operation. Dr. Williams and my Dad held me while the operation was performed in our home on a table.

I was not what you would call a healthy child until I reached my teens. When I was seven years old, I had typhoid-malaria fever that stayed with me for about two years, after which I became a skinny country boy. When a spell of malaria struck me, I would sit by the kitchen stove with my coat on and shake like an Aspen, even though the outside temperature was 100 degrees in the shade. Some days I would eat like a horse, and then for the next few days I wouldn't eat enough to keep a bird alive. That's malaria!

The house I was born in was built by my Grandpa Miller about 1860. It was of wood frame construction, the front being two-story with a one-story kitchen to which a summer-kitchen was attached, making it an L-shape. One of the front rooms was known as Grandma's room. Most of the furniture in this room belonged to her. It consisted of a wardrobe, bureau, double bed, a washstand with pitcher and bowl, a stove for heat, several rockers, a center table and an old-fashioned sewing basket. Around the walls of Grandma's room hanged several holy pictures, plus the pictures of Grandpa and Grandma Miller. Hers was the first bed I had seen with springs. We had a tick filled with corn shucks and a feather bed on top of that.

The other front room was where Mother and Dad and some of the children slept. It had two double beds, the cradle, several chairs and a round table that could be extended to seat a dozen people. On a shelf stood the faithful clock. In the winter there was also a big wood-burning stove. Both rooms had wall-to-wall rag carpeting. Around the wall hung the usual holy pictures. In one corner stood a big walnut wardrobe. Since there was usually a baby it slept in the cradle, while the next two older children slept in one of the double beds. The rest of the children slept upstairs. There was no heat or light upstairs, so we snuggled under a pure wool blanket with some homemade quilts and a heavy comforter (also homemade) on top of the blanket. Sometimes the holy water fountain was frozen all week. We always left our shoes in the kitchen, to keep them from freezing. Rubbers or goulashes for children were unknown in those days.

The kitchen was fourteen by sixteen feet although much of this was taken up by the stairs to the upper rooms. In it were the cook stove with its large workbox, a china cabinet, a dining table and a small table on which stood the cedar water pail with its glistening brass hoops. The spiders or skillet and some of the other cooking utensils hung on a rack on the wall. A kerosene lamp sat in a bracket which was also attached to the wall to keep it out of the children's reach. Above the dining table, on the wall, hung three holy pictures. In back of the door was a rack upon which the men hung their working coats, hats, and caps. Under the stairs was a closet in which was the bread-box, the boot-jack, the broom, the shoe brush and usually a mouse trap, which was my job to keep baited and set, as we had these pests the year round.

We cooked in the winter-kitchen, as we called it, from November to about April when we moved everything but the china cabinet out into the summer kitchen. That was always quite an occasion. The older ones helped with the stove and the dining table and the smaller children helped with the lighter items. Once the stove was set up, Mother and we children did the rest. The summer-kitchen was also fourteen by sixteen feet. Here we had what was then called a safe. It was similar to the china cabinet but instead of having glass or wood in the paneling it had tin in which were stamped decorative designs. These were stamped just deep enough to break through the metal, causing a small crack to allow air to circulate through. Although we had a screen door and screens on the windows there were always flies, no matter how hard we tried.

On rainy days or during a storm you could hear the raindrops hit the old clap-board roof and see the water run off the end as there were no gutters. Many times, I listened to the mud wasps build their mud nests on the rafters overhead. A wooden fence separated the yard from the barn lot over which the chickens could fly with ease. One year we had a hen which laid one egg daily in back of the summer-kitchen door. She would sneak in slowly and then go behind the door, always scratching a few times as though she were preparing a nest, although there was nothing but the bare floor. In about a half hour she would come out crackling and sure enough there was an egg, ready for the pan.

In front of the house there were two cedar trees. This seemed to be a must with the German people in that whole area. There were no evergreen trees in the woods anywhere, but every farmhouse had those two cedar trees. Besides the cedars we had three plum trees, a grape arbor to the front gate, a snowball bush, and several rose bushes in the front yard. There were no lawn mowers in those days, so the grass was cut with a sickle. The path under the grape arbor was kept clean of grass at all times. This was done by scraping it with a hoe several times during the summer. Usually, my sister Mary took care of that and it was usually done on Saturday so it would look nice on Sunday, when the people passed on their way to church. Oh yes! Most farmers were plenty proud of their places.

The smokehouse stood about twenty feet from the summer kitchen and in this part of the yard stood two cherry trees. Under the one was a big block of wood on which were the washbasins where we washed in the summer, and the towel, comb case, and mirror were on the porch close by. At the end of the porch stood the rain barrel where Mother caught rainwater for washing clothes, if it rained. In the smokehouse we kept the meat, lard, and the washing machine.

A picket fence separated the yard from the garden where Mother raised the summer vegetables; lettuce, radishes, beans, peas, cucumbers, tomatoes, cabbage, garlic, carrots, beets, onions, turnips, butter-beans, sweet potatoes, and endive in the fall. There was also catnip, sage, parsley, and quite a variety of flowers such as morning glories, bleeding heart, peony, poppy, Easter lilies, lady slippers, sunflowers, and a big white rose bush.

Mother had her own hot bed where she raised her own cabbage and tomato plants, along with the sweet potatoes. This was quite a job to do. First of all, the old ground had to be taken out, then about six inches of fresh stable manure was put in, upon which Mother put several gallons of boiling water. This helped to retain the heat. Then, the ground was put back as much as needed and the seeds placed just so. These were covered with some very rotten wood which we gathered from old logs and stumps. It was similar to peat moss and served the same purpose. After this a window was put in place and covered with some old blankets. On nice sunny days these were removed to let the sun hit the glass and warm the inside. While there was danger of frost, the blankets were replaced at night. In a week, the little plants began to appear above the ground and by the time the danger of frost had passed, they were large enough to transplant. The sweet potatoes were put in a little later. There was always something to do on the farm.

GRANDMOTHER MILLER

Let me start by telling you a little story about my Father's family. My Dad was the oldest child. Grandfather Miller was ten years older than Grandma Miller. They were married when Grandma was about eighteen years of age.

When my Father was seventeen years old, Cholera broke out in the neighborhood in August 1873, and after two weeks over thirty people in the area had died. Among these were my Grandfather, four of my Father's brothers and three of his uncles. Six of these people died in my Father's house. So, in two weeks my Grandmother's family of eight was reduced to three, one of which was a son about two years old. This son died the following month, so she was all alone with my Dad, a lad of seventeen.

Since my Dad was too young to take over the farm, my Grandmother rented the farm to an uncle of mine and started to keep house for a priest in St. Wendel, which was her parish. My Father found work with a farmer in the neighborhood and worked for him until he had earned enough money to pay off a small debt my Grandfather had with him. After that he worked in a sawmill in Kentucky and several other places until he was twenty-one years old. Then, he and Mother were married on November 27, 1877.

Grandma usually came for a visit about once a year. It was then that she used her room. We were always glad to see her come as that meant a little present and candy or cookies. For as long as I can remember she kept house for a priest in Ridgeway, Illinois. This was only about eighty miles, but she had to ride three different trains and it took her all day to make the trip. No jets in those days. Grandma was bothered with sick headaches and every time she came home it took a couple of days in bed and taking pills to get over the effect of the trip. I can still see Mother going to Grandma's room with a cup of hot coffee and some pills.

What I disliked about Grandma's homecoming was that first meeting. She would always insist on kissing us and how I hated to be kissed. The first graham crackers I ever ate were brought home by her. They were in a red box by Nabisco and were they ever good. We each got one. Once she also brought home a bottle of good wine but we didn't get much of that; it was for Dad.

I'll never forget the day she made biscuits for supper. Dad, Mother, and my brother Joe were hauling in hay and Grandma was baby-sitting and made supper. At that time the men had a game played by pitching silver dollars in a hole in the ground, something on the order of pitching horseshoes. Grandma's biscuits didn't raise and so they were thin like cookies. At the supper table I was sitting close to Dad and after taking one of the biscuits I said, "Dad, these would make good pitching dollars!" Dad sort of smiled and Grandma looked daggers at me. Poor Grandma.

Grandma was mighty good to us. She always bought Mary hats, and many times she sent home yard goods for dresses for Mary and Mother. She also sent five dollars for the children for Christmas and had to work hard for the money. I still have a rosary which she sent me in the year 1912 after they had a mission in her parish. I also have a picture which sat on her bureau while she was still alive. Grandma was the first person I saw wearing false dentures.

One Sunday, after church, a friend told Dad that he brought a box from Grandma. She was living in Ridgeway at that time, keeping house for Fr. Rensman. When we opened the box, it contained a Gem Roller Organ. Boy, that was something! Real music in the house! It was played by placing a wooden roller with many small pins, between two pins and turning the crank. By gliding over stops, the little pins opened them, allowing the air to escape and sound that note. The roll made three complete turns for one piece of music. We had thirteen rolls, which played such tunes as "Little Anne Ronnie", "Hail, Columbia", "Devil's Dream", "Marching Through Georgia", "Home Sweet Home", and several others. People came to visit us just to hear the music, since it was the first one around.

About six years later, we had the first phonograph or talking machine, as they were called then, so we gave the organ to the church to be raffled off at the social. A Mrs. John Pepper won it for twenty cents and was she glad, as it was still like new. We were not allowed to play the organ or phonograph during Lent. No music was allowed, nor was the organ in church played. The choir sang without music.

We had lots of visitors after we had the phonograph, as that was something new. It was a Columbia Phonograph Machine. The records were single side, and came in two sizes, seven and ten inches in diameter. The price for a record was twenty cents for a seven-inch, and one dollar for the ten-inch. We had about eighteen records of band and orchestra music. We also had some singing and a couple of the talking variety. We kids were not allowed to tough the machine. Dad or Mary took care of it. It was the only one for miles around and meant as much to us as do the modern hi-fi sets today. In fact, it was a more modern innovation as it was something completely new, while radio, television, and modern record players have been on the current market for quite some time. It was something to talk about, yes ma'am!

For a while, Grandma was housekeeper for a Father Donnenhoefer, and he was a good friend of the family. When I was born, someone suggested that Fr. be my godfather by proxy. His first name was Aloysius, so I received the middle name of Aloysius, hence, John A. Miller. Grandfather and Grandmother Schmitt were my sponsors, or godparents, with Grandfather standing in for Father Donnenhoefer. I remember seeing him once when I was seven years old. I was at school and Joe came and got me so Father could see me. He was a rather large man; I'd say about 200 pounds. He gave me a five-dollar gold piece and gave Dad a scolding for sending me to a public school.

Grandma continued to keep home for priests until the fall of 1914, when she came home to die, as she put it. She lived for another thirteen years and died just twenty-eight days short of her 90th birthday.

EARLY RECOLLECTIONS

By the time I was four years of age, Mother had had seven children. Joe was the oldest, almost seven years my senior. Next came my sister, Mary, who was two years younger than Joe, then Aloysius, who died at thirty-three months. Then came Frank, who was four and a half years older than I, then Adam, who died a week before my birth at twenty-six months. Finally came Rose, who was the baby at that time.

I can still remember the color of the last baby dress I wore. It was a lemon yellow with little figures that looked like musical notes. Since Mother had plenty to do with the cooking, sewing, milking, washing, and often times helping in the fields, it was pretty much up to Mary to take care of us, especially in keeping our hands and faces clean. Have you ever seen a little boy who likes to have his face washed by his sister when he was deeply interested in play? I was no different than most boys, so sometimes Mary had to put me in the highchair and use a little persuasion to get the job done. Usually, a word from Mother settled the difficulty.

Saturday, July 19, 1902, was a hot day. Joe and I had been working in the field across the road from the house. On our way home for lunch we met Dr. Whiting who informed us at about ten o'clock in the morning, a little brother had been born to us and that Mother and the baby were both fine. I was twelve years old then.

The baby was named Clements Adam. Uncle Adam and Aunt Mary were the sponsors. The little fellow grew like all babies and was a great source of enjoyment to the whole family.

February 2, 1903, started out as a pleasant Monday. It was nice and warm for that time of the year, and men went without their coats that day. In the afternoon, though, it began to rain. Dad had bought a team of mules from Julious Zenthoefer that morning and needed a collar for one of them. So, in the afternoon, when he and Frank drove to St. Wendel to but that collar, they picked us up after school. By the time we got home we were quite damp, as the umbrellas didn't protect us completely. Our wet clothes were hung by the kitchen stove to dry out.

Because of the damp weather, my little brother, Clements, became sick the next morning. Dad got Dr. Whiting, and for about

15

ten days he was very ill. On Sunday, February 15, Clements showed signs of improvement and we thought the crisis had passed, but on the morning on the 16th, it began to snow. I went to school alone that morning and Mother made me wear her over-shoes. The weather turned into a regular blizzard, blowing the fine snow through the cracks and underneath the windows. The temperature dropped to zero. This caused my little brother to have a relapse. The next day, on Friday, February 17, 1902, at seven o'clock in the morning, little Clements was taken to heaven.

Because of the severe weather, I stayed the night of the 16th with the Waszmer family, just across the road from our school. I slept in a little room off the kitchen, without fire and without heat. The next morning, my shoes were frozen stiff. I had to thaw them out in the oven before I could wear them. About nine o'clock that morning, during school recess, I was startled when my Dad laid his hand on my shoulder. I was skating during recess, even though I had been told not too, for fear I might fall and break a bone. I was expecting a reprimand. Instead, I was told to tell the Sister that I was going home since my baby brother had died that morning. Dad asked me to wait at Raben's Store while he and Uncle Adam went to the undertaker to get a little casket for our baby. Instead of waiting, I told Mr. Raben to tell my Father that I had gone home with a neighbor.

When I came in the house, my Mother was sitting in a rocking chair by the stove, crying. She told me to go into Grandma's room where our baby was laid out on a wide board, until Dad brought the little casket home. Two days later, Clements was buried in St. Wendel Cemetery. As the little casket was lowered into the grave, my Mother, with a little wave of her hand, said in a low tone, "Goodbye, Clemie", and we left him to God. This was the third baby my parents had followed to the grave in this Cemetery. It wasn't easy.

It seems as though the 'sevens' had dominated with Clements. He was the seventh son, was seven months old, died on the 17th at seven in the morning, while the temperature was seven below zero.

Father had an Aunt Katharina. She was a sister of Grandpa Miller and the widow of Wendel Waszmer after whom St. Wendel was named. While she was living, we went to see her once a year during the summer. Father would put some hay in the bottom of the wagon for the children to sit on. Then, on a Sunday morning, we all dressed in our Sunday best and started out for her house, which was just across the road from the school yard. Aunt Katharina had two old-maid daughters who were dress-makers and lived at home with her. Mother, Dad, and the older children would go to Mass while one of the girls took care of the younger children. Aunt Katharina had one bad eye that watered constantly, and since she did not wear glasses it looked bad. She was always very inquisitive. She would lure me over to her chair and then lock me with her legs and hold me tight until she received from me the answers to her questions. Sometimes I should have invoked the Fifth Amendment as some of her inquiries were rather tricky and with my parents in the same room waiting for my answers I often had a cold sweat coming on by the time I was released. We always had two meals and about an hour before sundown we started for home. They were real good to us with plenty to eat, if only they hadn't asked so many questions.

Since we lived three miles from church and there was always a baby to care for, Mother and Mary alternated in going to Mass. When we saw Grandpa Schmitt go by from church it was time to put the potatoes on the fire so they would be done by the time the men folk had finished with the chores. I used to watch for Grandpa, since he and Grandma had a small express or spring wagon, as they were called by some people. Grandpa drove a white horse, so they were easy to see coming down the road.

Father and Mother weren't very prosperous the first few years of their married life. With the death of two children, my operation, doctor bills, and accidents with horses, they were in debt for some time. I remember my Father talking about the interest being due to a Mr. Stein on some money Father had borrowed from him.

Father and Mother both worked very hard. The fences were all in a very bad condition and Dad had to split rails and pickets and posts to replace them, so he could keep the cows and pigs in the fields. He also cleared forty acres of wooded area and that is extremely hard work. He couldn't afford to pay adult wages, so he usually had a boy about fourteen years old as a helper. This meant that all the heavy work had to be done by Dad. I watched him split pickets and it's quite a trick to get them straight. Once he and Joe were putting up a new fence and Joe was digging the holes for the posts. When he had dug the hole about two and a half feet deep, he dug up a snake that had not as yet come out of the ground for the summer. I helped set up rail fences when I was still too small to reach high enough to put on the last two or three rails. It's a dirty job on a windy day as the loose dirt blows into your eyes no matter how hard you try to avoid it. Some wasps and hornets make their nests from this loose wood dirt. They combine it with saliva from their mouth and when it is dry its stronger than cloth.

I was a great one to make fires around old rotten stumps, even when I was just a wee shaver. At that time there still were some stumps in most of our fields and whenever Dad or Joe were plowing in these fields, I would beg them to let me start a fire on a stump. I would carry wood from wherever I could find it to keep the fire going. No, I was never burned, as I was very careful with matches and around fire.

When Dad was cutting wheat, I would walk behind the binder for a few times around the field until I got tired. It was great fun for me to watch the wheat being carried up to the binding machinery that tied it into bundles. I usually did this after lunch which was at nine o'clock in the morning. Mother would send Frank and I with a cool jug of water, some bread, jelly, or some kind of preserves and they would spread it on the bread themselves. Never any sandwiches. This was enough to keep them going until dinner.

I remember when the big wheel on the binder dropped into a ditch and we had to borrow a shovel from a neighbor, which was closer than our house, and dig a trench so the horses could pull the binder out of the hole.

About two weeks after the wheat was cut, it was hauled home and put in large stacks where it sat for about six weeks until it was trashed. If it was left in the fields it would get wet and rot, while in the stacks it would stay dry. One of my Dad's cousins always did the stacking and he was very good at it. He had a way of placing those bundles of wheat so that the rain would run off like water on a duck's back. I can still see him sitting on our back porch and singing German songs to me while waiting for Mother to call us for dinner. I enjoyed hearing him and Dad talk about the things they did when they were young men. It was a lot different from what the kids talk about today. I can still smell the fired ham, boiled potatoes, a big dish of lettuce, or sliced tomatoes and cucumbers, fresh from the garden. Then there was always some kind of pie; apple, blackberry, custard, or maybe peach. Mmmmmmmm!

Haying time was tough on us kids. Joe would pitch the hay into the loft, Dad and Mother would throw it back, and we kids had to tramp it down. Does it ever get hot in a hay loft under an old clapboard roof when the temperature is 100 degrees outside! Everyone had to help. I helped plant potatoes when I was too small to carry a full pail, so I took a half pail instead.

Another hot job is picking blueberries along some old rail fence. We went almost a half mile to an old abandoned farm where they had grown. We never took any water along as we had enough to carry if we were lucky to get there before someone else got them. On a good day we would come home with five or six gallons of berries. Along with the heat there were plenty of insect bites and scratches. On one of these days, Frank and I wanted to cross a little creek when we came upon the largest snake I ever saw in the open. We first decided to kill it so we found a big club, but when we came back and took another look we decided the snake was too big for us to tackle, so we walked away and left it all coiled up in a heap. It was quite a job to get those wild blackberries, but the eating well compensated us for our trouble; preserves, jelly, pies, and just plain canned to eat with potato pancakes.

We had two walnut trees on our farm and one year, Frank and I gathered up and peeled over a bushel of walnuts. It's a messy job as the walnut juice stains your hands and it's impossible to wash it off. It takes a week or more to get completely rid of it. Dad took the nuts along to town and Mrs. Cooper gave him about sixty cents for the whole lot. Rose and I got a knife and fork from the dime store, plus a few pennies, while Frank took his share in money, about twenty-five cents. You had to do a lot of work then to earn a quarter. We also had a mulberry and a persimmon tree on our farm. Mulberries ripen in the summer while persimmons are not good to eat until we have a good frost, which was around November 1st. We used to take a tin pail and get some to eat. Mulberries are very sweet while persimmons have a taste all their own. We used to make a cider with them. It looks just like champagne, although it is not intoxicating, and tastes very good.

While he had the old stable and barn, mud-swallows would build their nests up against the rafters. It was interesting to watch them plaster the mud and make a nest with just a little hole for them to enter. Sometimes a sparrow would come near but he was quickly driven off. They came in the spring and left again in the fall, like they do at Capistrano, California. After the old stable and barn were torn down, they never returned. We all missed them.

In the summertime, we children always went barefoot all week. By Sunday, our feet were so spread out that we had difficulty putting our shoes on. How we ran all over without cutting our feet to pieces was amazing. Once in a while we picked up a thorn and had to sit down to remove it, but that was about all. Once I cut my foot while cutting corn, but some home remedies soon healed it up again. It was a lot of fun to get out after a thunderstorm and run around in the mud and water, like Huckleberry Finn and Tom Sawyer.

We usually had one or two cardinals in a cage. Joe would make a cardinal trap with corn stalks and set it down by the creek. He would bait it with corn and when the snow was deep the cardinals would go after the corn and get caught in the trap. They had no game laws or game wardens then and you could trap wild animals or birds and keep them as pets. On some days, these cardinals would sing their heads off, while on other days they wouldn't give out a peep. Dad always said there would be a change in the weather when they did this.

We also had a little black and white rat terrier dog named Spunny. We had a lot of fun together. I usually carried a frog sticker. What's a frog sticker? It's an old rusty jack-knife with only a half blade and one or both of the handles missing. In the fall when the turnips were large enough to eat, I would get one, wash and peel it, then sit on the stoop by the summer-kitchen, and Spunny and I would eat it. Every time I cut a bite for myself, I also cut one for him, and did he like turnips. Once I played a dirty trick on him. Mother had some coffee cake that was sort of stale, so she sliced it in a bread pan and in the oven to toast it a little. Spunny and I were sitting by the stove and Mother told me to remind her of the cake so it wouldn't burn. You guessed right; we both forgot, and it was burned to a charcoal black. Mother gave me a scolding for forgetting so I touched Spunny's paw to the hot stove. I got a sound slap for it, which I deserved. The poor dog wasn't to blame.

I suppose you wonder what we kids did for fun and entertainment, as we had no store toys to play with. In the spring, Dad would get a load of yellow sand from the creek and dump it in our playpen where we usually played in the morning. We would use empty sardine cans for wagons, and we would haul this sand in what we called a field and spread it evenly. Then we would cup it with both hands which raised it in little mounds resembling wheat shocks, which was what it was supposed to be. Then we would haul it again and let it run down a board which we had tilted up with a rock or stick and it would pile up to look like a new straw stack just after they finished trashing wheat. We would do this over and over until we got tired of it. Then we would play horse by tying a string, which were the reins, on each arm. This way we would go to town or to church or whatever struck our fancy. If we had a wagon, we would pull it along and if not, we made believe and went without. We had regular roads in the barn-lot over which we passed, and each led to an imaginary place. There is a weed that grew in Indiana which, if trimmed right, resembles a well clipped mules' tail. These we would take and carry in front of us and make-believe we were driving a team of mules. Oh, it was a lot of fun to play make-believe with almost anything. With big spikes and clothes pins for people and a few scraps of cloth for quilts, we played for hours putting them to bed and getting them up again in the morning and off to work and the kids off to school. In the afternoon, when the weather was good, we always played in the shade of the granary. We played school, house, or whatever came to our minds. About three o-clock in the summer, if the men were working in the fields, I had to bring them a jug of fresh water. Before the new barn was built, we played a lot in the old barn and the old stable. It was nice and cool in the driveway of the old barn.

Our horse stable had an overhanging roof and here we often played during the rain, blocking the water with corncobs and hayseed from the manger. When the water backed up until it was about to run into the stable, we would break the dam and make-believe that a flood was sweeping down across the valley, carrying along with it the corncobs and debris like a regular flood does in some places in the spring. Imagination played a major part in our amusements when we were children.

It seemed that after Teddy Roosevelt stormed San Juan Hill in Cuba with his Rough Riders, every farm boy who could sit on a horse believed himself to be a Rough Rider. One night, about nine o'clock at night, after we had all retired, two neighbor boys rode by. They let out a western war-hoop and shouted, "Two Rough Riders!"

Joe woke up and said, "Yea . . . two damn fool Rough Riders!" Joe hated to be woke up by such shenanigans, as he called them.

Close to the old stable was an elderberry bush. Some of these would get quite large, and when the inside is removed, they have a hole as large as a lead pencil, some even larger. In the winter, we would make popguns with them. Most boys in school had one. We would make a plunger, or ramrod, with a tough piece of hickory wood, and chew paper wads for bullets. They made quite a loud pop if you knew how to load and shoot them. They were really dangerous, as they had the power to knock out a windowpane or an eye if you made a direct hit. One day, a boy loaded his popgun in school and somehow it went off. The wad landed on Sister's desk, and the gun landed in the stove. We used to play rabbits and hounds as we were usually too far away to hit anybody. It was lots of fun, though.

Nothing fascinated me like running water in a ditch or creek, or fire on an old stump or brush pile. I loved to walk alongside a ditch or creek to watch the water as it ran over stones and gravel and listen to its rippling sounds. I did this many times and, sometimes, picked up an arrowhead once used by some Indian long ago.

When I was still quite young, Joe was getting a small farm paper in which there were all kinds of advertisements for puzzles, dream books, cheap pens, etc. One ad was for a camera that was supposed to take real pictures. All you had to do was send in twenty cents with your name and address. Frank and I pooled our money and sent for it. I was going to school then, and as the post office was in Raben's Store, I checked for the mail on my way home from school. One night, he gave me a package addressed to me. I opened it and in it was our camera. What a laugh! It was a little black box with the head of a thumb-tack protruding through one end. If you pushed on the head, it raised a little folder about the size of a matchbox. Inside of this folder were two pictures of a jackass with an inscription below which read, "When shall we three meet again?" Get it? We had a lot of fun with this little black box, for no matter who came to the house, we took their picture. I took it along to school and everybody wanted their picture taken with it.

Once, Joe received a baseball bat with a suit of clothes. On Sunday afternoon, he would bat the ball and we kids would run retrieve it for him. The roof on the old stable was quite low and it was easy for Joe to drive the ball over the roof into the lot behind the stable. To get a turn at bat, you had to be able to catch the ball. One Sunday afternoon, our neighbor walked by and asked to join in on the fun. He batted the ball a few times, but Joe had the bat most of the time, while Mr. Spahn was helping us retrieve the ball. He told us later that he was so stiff the next morning that he couldn't get up to do his chores. He was quite a bit older than us kids and not use to chasing balls. We used home-made balls made with yarn that we obtained by unraveling old socks. We usually put a walnut inside which made the ball travel better.

Once, Joe and Frank, with some help from Dad, played a dirty trick on me. They introduced me to go on a snipe hunt. If you don't know what a snipe hunt is, let me tell you that it is a fake, and many people have been fooled by this. Oh, it's lots of fun for those who do the fooling, but not so nice for the victim. A snipe, or dil-dappa, as they were called by the German's, is supposed to be a fabulous animal and a very good one to eat. Anyway, here is how it's done. The victim is taken for a ride out a good ways from town and is given a large bag. This bag he is to hold in a certain way, and the gang that goes with him will scare up the snipe and chase them into the bag. After this, they will all join the feast of cooking and eating them. After the victim is all set with the bag, the gang go off in a direction where the snipe are supposed to be congregating to chase them into the bag. What they actually do is go back to the rig or car and go back to town, leaving the victim holding the bag. After an hour or so, the victim finally gets wise that he has been duped, and in disgust, walks back to town. Of course, the gang are all on the lookout for him and make all kinds of excuses as to why he didn't get any snipe, putting all the blame on him. Many a poor boob has made that long walk back to town to discover that he was the victim of a well laid plot and the laughingstock of the town. In my case, I was set in a fence corner not far from the barn, while my brothers were to chase the dil-dappa up from the creek. I was lucky, though, in that I saw my brothers going across the field towards home before they got there, so I didn't sit there very long waiting for the prey to appear. My Dad was standing up by the barn watching me and having a good laugh. As I said, it's lots of fun for everybody, except for the poor fool that is the victim.

For a long time, Mother bought Arbuckle Brothers Coffee. It was roasted and packed in one-pound packages. On one side was a coupon with the Arbuckle brothers on it. These were good for prizes. I saved them for a long time and then sent for a premium catalog. I send for a Noah's Ark. This consisted of a dozen pair of cardboard animals, male and female. They were held together so they could be opened and would stand on a table or on the floor. I don't know if I remember all of the animals, but there were cats, dogs, tigers, bears, pigs, lions, zebras, cows, horses, elephants, and giraffes. They were very nice, and I appreciated these pieces of cardboard as much as a kid today appreciates a new bike. I still had them when my brother Henry got old enough to play with them, and he also had a lot of enjoyment with them. Children in those days valued such things and took very good care of them so they lasted for many years.

I always liked machinery or anything with turning wheels. Since I had nothing like that to play with, I would take empty thread spools and mount them with a long nail on the side of the old barn. With string for belts and, using the grindstone for the engine, I would set the spools spinning, making believe it was a thrashing machine. A few empty spools, some string, and a lot of imagination created a powerful machine and a lot of pastime.

When I was a little fellow, there were a lot of peddlers, as we called them. They would go from house to house trying to sell some kind of kitchen gadget, horse liniment, salve, cheap jewelry, linens, or what have you. Some would walk while others had a horse and rig. One such peddler was a Mr. Goldschmitt. He had a yellow beard and a yellow horse and rig. He sold some kind of liniment. He usually arranged it so he would arrive at our place about sundown and then ask to stay all night. My parents were very considerate with fellows like him and they didn't mind giving him a nights lodging and feed for his horse. In the morning he offered to pay but Dad always refused to take anything. He was quite a storyteller and had a high-pitched voice when he laughed. I still remember one story he used to tell. It seems he met this fortune teller and this lady told him a lot of things about the past and the future and when she got all through, he asked her if she knew everything. When she told him she did he replied, "Then you should have known that I just came in here to make a fool out of you!" He was quite a character.

Another old man by the name of Geldreich use to stop at our house twice a year, in the spring and late summer. All he would eat was bread and milk. When he came, Mother would get a crock of milk and a large loaf of bread and the butcher knife and told him to help himself, which he did. He was a very skinny man, about fifty years old. When he was younger, he and his oldest son went to the village, and when they returned they found the rest of his family, his wife and three children, had been murdered. In trying to find the murderers he spent all he possessed. and when he didn't find them, he just started to wander from place to place and get a handout whenever he could. He looked pitiful.

Sometimes, Gypsies would stop to buy something from us, like bacon, eggs, or maybe some vegetables. They offered to pay by telling Mother her fortune. Of course, she didn't believe in that, so they always got what they wanted for free. Mother was always glad to get rid of them as people were afraid of Gypsies and gave them what they wanted.

I must tell you about the time an Italian peddler stopped at our place. While he was talking to Mother and Joe, trying to make a sale, he rolled a cigarette and after smoking it a while, he threw it on the ground. I picked it up and took a puff. Boy, did I get heck that time, both from Mother and Joe.

Those poor peddlers would carry two grips all day in that hot sun. I don't see how they could do it as the two grips must have weighed close to one hundred pounds. One grip was a telescope type where they had their linens, tablecloths, etc. The other was more like a small suitcase. In this they had combs, safety pins, needles, pencils, a razor or two and numerous sundries. It was a mighty hard grind.

I always liked company and was glad to see someone come to visit. Grandpa Schmitt, two of my uncles, and Dad took turns going to Evansville with the butter and what produce we had to sell. Each went about one week apart. Whenever one went to town, he would notify the others the day before so they could bring whatever they had to send to Mrs. Cooper, where it was bartered for groceries and staples. Very little money was ever exchanged here. They would bring their things with a list of the groceries they wanted the evening before, and the next day all was taken care of. Dad packed all the eggs in sawdust filled boxes to keep them from breaking as farm wagons had no springs and riding in them was pretty jolting. They received about ten to fifteen cents for a pound of butter and about the same for a dozen of eggs. It depended on the time of the year.

Sugar was selling for five cents a pound, non-roasted coffee was twelve cents a pound, while roasted coffee was two cents higher. Mother usually saved the two cents and roasted her own. A large box of mustard sardines was ten cents, or three boxes foe a quarter. A twenty-pound box of soda crackers sold for one dollar. Most items were sold in bulk form.

I enjoyed listening to the jokes told by Grandpa and the uncles. Mother use to laugh until the tears ran down her cheeks, but when Grandpa started on those German ghost stories, that was entirely different. Sometimes my hair would stand on end, they were so weird. Grandpa could speak, read, and write German, French, and English. He also transcribed music and was the leader of the church choir. I was about four years old when Grandma and Grandpa celebrated their Golden Wedding Anniversary. It started with a Mass and Blessing, after which we went to Grandpa's house for the day. Their children bought for each a large rocker which was decorated with a wide yellow ribbon. Grandma had a new lavender dress trimmed with gold braid. It was fun going to their house as Grandma always had cookies with red sugar on them and she often had candy too. I loved a piece of her bread with peach preserves on it. She used a spice called coriander, which gave it a real good taste. Dad didn't like the taste, so mother never used it. Like most Germans, Grandma raised geese and we children had to be careful as those big ganders could really fight and hurt you, especially when there were goslings around.

Grandpa died in April of 1896, while Grandma lived until November 1900. They came to this country around 1855 from somewhere near Strasbourg, Alsac-Lorain, with one daughter and three sons. The daughter took sick and died and was buried at sea. I still have a wooden matchbox and a crucifix which they brought from over the seas.

Whenever we went somewhere it was quite a job to get all the children ready, especially the girls, with their three or four petticoats all starched and ironed to perfection. When they walked by it sounded like a mild storm approaching. Mary usually took care of the older ones, while Mother would see to the baby. Everything had to be just so. On Saturday, all the shoes were shined to make sure they looked their best. Those days we all wore ankle length button shoes except Dad. He wore what was called a gaiter shoe. It had no buttons or lace. The top had elastic on each side which allowed the foot to slide in and keep the shoe from coming off. Mother always wore her wedding dress on such occasions unless the weather was very warm. The dress was made in two pieces of a heavy brown material. With it she wore a small bustle which was quite in style then. She also wore a genuine garnet necklace with a gold cross. It was a heirloom which Grandma had brought from Germany and was very beautiful.

On the way to Grandpa's house we passed Mr. Schweikhart's house and always looked for his peacock. Sometimes we would see him with his tail spread out like a fan and was it ever beautiful. He would strut his stuff before the rest of the barnyard fowl. It still amuses me to think back over those days and in my mind picture some of the events of my boyhood. Those were the "Gay Nineties" when most people on the farm had little more than a living, a lot of hard work, and high hopes for the future.

I recall Dad telling about helping to raise the Campaign Pole in St. Wendel during a presidential election year. The area around St. Wendel was a strong Democrat region so they raised the Democratic Pole there, on top of which was a rooster. The Lutheran area, south of St. Wendel, was mostly Republican, so the Republican Pole was raised at Blairsville. There was a great rivalry between these two areas, with each wanting to have the tallest pole, so they were often over a hundred feet tall. They were made by splicing tree trunks together, and were raised by means of a construction boom, horses, and a heavy block and tackle. The Republican Pole was crowned with an eagle. At the base of the pole was a platform from which the candidates made their campaign speeches and promises. Since St. Wendel was half in Posey County and half in Vanderburg County, candidates from both counties campaigned there. Most of the candidates were seeking some county office, but once in a while, a candidate for a state office would also come there for a rally, as they were called. If the candidate came for an evening rally, he might be met at the train station by a torch-light parade of mounted men, each carrying a lighted kerosene torch. That was really something. The beer at the saloon's flowed in abundance and everybody had a good time, whether they intended to vote for the man or not. Since the candidates picked up the tab, the saloon owners got their contribution towards a pole back, a hundred-fold! I don't remember a campaign pole in my day, but they had them in earlier years. I do remember political rallies at St. Wendel, but I was still much too young to attend any of them. When I was born, Benjamin Harrison, a Republican, was President of the United States.

CHICAGO WORLD'S FAIR, 1893

In the later part of October 1893, my Dad, uncle, and cousin left for Chicago to attend the Columbia World's Fair. The United States Mint produced a half-dollar piece which had the head of Christopher Columbus on it and was known as the Colombian Half-Dollar, in commemoration of the World's Fair and the four-hundredth anniversary of the discovery of America. I was four years old then.

I believe the roundtrip railroad fare to Chicago was only five dollars; a little less than one cent per mile. When Dad came home and told us about the things he had seen there it sounded incredible. Buildings thirty stories high. We thought we were up high when we looked out of the upstairs window, but thirty stories! Wow, that was really something. To hear about the things they saw at the Fair; machines that made nails faster than you could pick them up, a talking machine in the form of a man that told all about the qualities of a shoe for men. Dad brought home a postcard with the message that this man/machine gave concerning the shoe. It was called HupCore and was a gaiter style shoe as those worn by my Dad. The fancy laces and clothing exhibited by European countries were modeled by beautiful women from their country. Dad said the prettiest women there were from the Scandinavian Provinces.

Dad talked about the bright streetlights and the cable cars on which they rode to and from the fair grounds. He talked about the Ferris Wheel over 150 feet tall that carried eight to ten people in each cab. This wheel was to the Chicago Fair what the Eiffel Tower was to Paris and the Space Needle to Seattle. No, our men didn't ride on it. They were too scared. One day something went wrong, and the Wheel didn't move for over two hours. The people on it were trapped up in the air for all that time. It was rumored that when it resumed operation, an old lady was found dead in one of the cabs. She apparently died from fright.

They went down the Midway and paid a dime to see a horse that had his head where the tail should be and vice-versa. When they got into the tent, they saw a horse in a very narrow stall backed in against a manger filled with oats and hay, so that its head was facing out instead of its rear. Get it? It was the gospel truth and it brought in a lot of dimes, especially from the farmers. What a laugh!

On the south side of Jefferson Avenue in Detroit, just west of the Belle Isle Bridge, stands a large stove. It was made for and exhibited at The Chicago Fair. As a coincidence, my wife's Uncle Remi helped to make that stove. Dad brought home a postcard describing this stove.

They also toured the Sears-Roebuck Plant. It was then a single building covering a whole block and stood about six stories tall. Dad brought home one of their catalogs (spelled catalogue then). Dad wasn't buying from them then, but that catalog was prized as a special possession and we had to get his permission to look at the pictures in it. It was in a cardboard tube and it had an exotic, sweet smell when the lid was opened. That catalog remained around our house for years and served as an amusement many times when we children were tired of playing. Nothing was ever ordered from it.

Dad also brought some little knickknacks and a basket of concord grapes. That was a real treat for us at that time of the year. How we use to sit and listen to have Dad tell some visitors all about the Fair. We were all ears. I am sure it was a real exciting experience to them, the same as it would be today for anyone who had never seen anything like it before. Just picture yourself being four years old, having never seen anything but the countryside between our farm and the church just three miles distant and you can get some idea of the thoughts that raced through my mind when I heard the things discussed by my Dad, yet, what would they be today, compared to the wonders that are on display in modern fairs.

SCHOOL DAYS

I started school in the fall of 1896 at School House No. 1, which was just three-quarters of a mile from our house. It was three miles to St. Wendel's and my parents thought it was too far for me to walk, so my first school experience was in a public school. Our teacher's name was Miss Alice Kaline. She was quite young but very nice. There were about eighteen pupils in all, ranging in ages from seven to fourteen years. There were more girls than boys, but we got along very well together. School started at nine o'clock in the morning with a twenty-minute recess at ten-thirty, one hour for lunch at noon, and a ten-minute recess in the afternoon, with dismissal as four o'clock.

Clear Creek was about one quarter mile from the school grounds, so some days we went fishing there during the noon hour. We played the usual games or went on a lizard hunt along the old rail fence that bordered the school grounds. If we killed any we buried them in one corner of the school yard.

One day, one of the older boys got the idea to burn off the grass in the school yard. All went well, and when the bell rang, all was under control and all the fire was out. I had one match left, known as a sulfur match. Its head was made of a sulfur compound and, when struck on some rough object, it would sort of glow and smoke before bursting into a flame. Sometimes they wouldn't burn at all. I struck this match on a piece of brick and when it didn't flame up after several seconds, I stuck it in a clump of grass thinking that it was out. Of course, it wasn't. After about twenty minutes one of the girls asked to be excused and when she opened the door, a fire started by my match was almost up to the schoolhouse. We all fought the fire and in a little while we had it out and the schoolhouse was saved. I got a scolding from the teacher, but as I hadn't done it on purpose, it wasn't too severe.

For lunch I carried some bread spread with jelly, preserves, or apple-butter, depending on what Mother had to offer. Usually a piece of pie, cake, or cookies was included. One day, these began to disappear from my lunch pail. When I accused an older boy for taking them, he denied it. One day I had a piece of berry pie stolen, and he forgot to wipe his mouth after eating it. I called the teacher again and when she confronted him with it, he admitted that he had been taking the things from my lunch pail. I had no more losses after that! The boy lived just a little way from school and in the afternoon, two older girls went to his house and told his mother what he had been doing, so he received his just punishment. He had been taking these things at recess while I was outside playing.

My school days ended at School House No. 1 in the spring of 1897 when I was stricken with Typhoid Malaria fever. I was very sick and for a few days my life hung in the balance. Fearing that I might die, my Dad got Father Heck and with his help I made my first confession. My Mother had briefed me before Father arrived and all went well. About this time Dad called in another doctor and after a joint consultation they changed my medicine and I began to improve. By this time I was so weak that I wasn't able to stand alone, but by daily sitting in a chair for short periods, I gradually gained strength to where I was able to walk to and from the chair. In time I was up and around again. It was then that the Malaria fever struck me. No matter how much medicine I took, it didn't seem to help. When a spell would hit me, I would shake like an Aspen. I would sit right next to the stove with a coat on, although it was 100 degrees outside, still cold and shivering. Some days I would eat enough for two boys, and then again, I wouldn't eat enough to keep a bird alive. That's what Malaria fever does to you. During the summer and through an old neighbor, my parents heard of a medicine made in Tennessee called "Dr. Kilmer's Swamp Root". After taking several bottles of this medicine, the fever left me, but I didn't go back to school until April of 1898.

This, however, doesn't mean that I had no schooling during this time. Not at all. I had a primer in both German and English and my parents saw to it that I studied these under the tutoring of my sister Mary. I also had Catechism from which I had to study every day and had to be committed to memory. I had a slate on, which I did my arithmetic and writing while the spelling was studied followed by an oral examination given to me by Mary. This also applied to my reading. If all the answers were correct my study period was over for the day. If not, I went back and studied until I could give all the correct answers. There was no fooling around in that school. If I per chance was a little out of order, Mother soon dispelled my behavior. This schooling paid off well when I started at Parochial school at St. Wendel's. Although I had only seven months of schooling at School House No. 1, I was able to do grade-two work in all subjects. I was almost nine years old now and had missed a whole year of schooling.

When I started back to school at St. Wendel, we had nuns for teachers and their discipline was a little stricter that the School House. We started the day with Mass at eight o'clock in the morning. The first subject was always Catechism, followed by German reading either from a reader or from the Bible, after which we had a twenty-minute recess. After the recess, we had arithmetic and sometimes some writing until noon. A one-hour lunch was followed by reading in English, after which came one or two of the following subjects: geography, English or German composition, spelling, history, grammar, and copybook writing exercises. While the days were still long, we had a short recess in the afternoon, and in winter we had no afternoon recess but were let out fifteen minutes earlier. It took us about an hour to walk home. Sometimes we left school at 3:15 in the winter and would take our time walking home. Once, the stars were already shining by the time we got home. When this happened, we got a good talking to by Dad with a threat of punishment if it happened again.

Rubbers or goulashes for children were unknown in those days, so we walked through the fields and woods when the roads were muddy. Sometimes our shoes looked like clumps of mud and it was quite a job to get them clean. In the winter, the stars were still shining when we left in the morning and with the temperature down to zero it was plenty cold to walk the three miles, especially if a cold east wind was blowing. I had no overcoat or sweater as these were not made in children's sizes back then. The only boys who owned sweaters were those who had a Grandma that could knit them one and I wasn't that fortunate. Most girls wore a large wool shawl folded in a triangle and fastened at the throat with a big safety pin. Few girls had coats. They kept their hands under the corners of their shawl, although they had a pair of mittens to help. These were usually a present from Grandma at Christmas time. For many years, Mother wore a shawl like that in winter and a lighter one when the weather got warmer. Later on she had a large cape, as did my sister Mary. Coats, or cloaks as they were known then, were only for the rich, as they were too costly for the average person.

For our school lunch we carried bread with jelly, preserves, or apple-butter spread on it. This depended on whether we had a good year for fruit. If not, homemade molasses took the place of anything else. Mother bought nothing at the store like that, in fact, there was nothing to buy except syrup which we didn't like, so molasses filled the bill. Sometimes a piece of ham, an egg, or during lent a piece of fish, was also in the pail. If apples or peaches were in season, we would have one, and quite often cake or pie was also included. Everybody carried their lunch in a two-quart tin pail with a lid made especially for this purpose. We crossed Clear Creek twice on our way and, one evening, one of the boys suggested that we put all of our dinner pails in the water hole and throw large clods of dried mud in the water to make the pails bob up and down. My cousin aimed wrong and hit my pail, putting a deep dent in it. I pushed it out as well as I could but not good enough. In washing the pail that night, my sister Mary noticed the dent and told Mother about it. My Dad was sitting close by and, being afraid that I would get a slap if I told the truth on how it happened, I lied and said I had fallen down. Shame on me!

We all used slates in those days and had a cigar box with a bottle of water and a cloth to clean the slates with. If we were in a hurry, a little spit and the handkerchief did the trick. It was a mess, but the boys did it that way. Oh no, not the girls!

One of our games during recess or lunch was baseball, but not as it is played today, as we used fewer players. We also played marbles, tag, and, in the winter, hare and hounds. We also had a game called daddy long-legs. For this game we would get a small boy and give him a large stick with the permission to whoop the daylights out of us if he could catch us. We had a little red-headed fellow whom we always selected if he would play. We had nick-named him Lightening, which infuriated him and that was the whole object of the game. He would try his best to catch us and, have no fear, he often did, and it would be woe to the one he caught. The only way to stop him was to grab the stick and get out of his way before he could strike again. It was lots of fun and we never had any hard feelings after the game was over. We never played cops and robbers and bang-bang like they do today. Children made up their own games then and had lots of fun playing them, I believe more so than they do today with all their modern toys and gadgets. It was a lot of fun those days to be a healthy boy or girl.

Our school was conducted on the merit system. The better you knew your lessons the more merits you could earn, and your report card was marked accordingly. On the first of the month you were moved up or down the seat row in accordance to the amount of merits you earned. A visitor could tell who the best students were by the seats they occupied. About once a month, Father Pfeiffer would come into the room, unannounced, to test us on our religious studies. He was very nice but also very exacting. He would walk up and down the aisle while explaining some subjects, and suddenly ask a question, which often no one could answer. If his back was turned, Sister would whisper the answer to the kids in the front row and one of them would raise their hand and give the answer. You might call it cheating, but it saved face for the Sister as she was supposed to have taught us these answers.

Corporal punishment was in order if the offense was severe. It was usually a couple of whacks across the palm of each hand. For minor infractions, we would have to write a task during recess, noon hour, or after school, depending as to when the deed was committed.

How I hated to get up in the morning to go to school, especially in the winter. No matter how much sleep I had, it never seemed enough. After a scolding for not getting up when called, I would resolve to do better, but the next morning, the spirit was willing, but the flesh was weak.

I brought three books home every night to study; English reading, German reading, and Catechism. These I carried in a home-made school bag slung over my shoulder. Our Catechism had to be committed to memory and if you didn't know it, you stayed in at recess and studied. If you couldn't recite it then, you had the lunch hour to study some more.

In the morning we usually walked to school alone, but in the evening the whole group walked together. We got along pretty well together, knowing full well what would happen at home if anything serious came up between us children. The older one's sort of watched over the little ones. If we had any lunch left in the evening, we usually exchanged what we had with each other, a sort of share the wealth plan. In hot weather all the boys went to school barefoot. It was the custom down there. Blue shirt, knee pants, and a straw hat, and in the winter a vest, coat, and a cap with earmuffs was added.

When I went to school, the St. Wendel Mill was still running about two days a week. We kids knew the engineer well, so about once a year, we would take a cut through the mill property to see it. We followed the little creek that ran from the mill pond to Clear Creek, until we came out to the road. Sometimes we cut through Jim Hayne's Woods. By doing this, we had to climb a hill that was so steep that we had to grab onto bushes to help us get to the top. Finally, we would stop at the engine house and watch the engine run for a little while. It was fascinating to see the large fly wheel turn and the steam puff out of the exhaust pipe, as the engine chucked along for a twelve-hour day. The old mill has been torn down a long time now, but I still can see that engine run. When the wind was coming from the east, we could hear the whistle at our house, three miles away. What memories I can conjure up when I relax and let my mind wander in the past.

I received my first Holy Communion on May 31, 1903 and that was the end of my schooling. I was now nearly fourteen years old and, as St. Paul said, I laid away the ways of a child and began taking on those of a man.

THE NEW BARN

In the fall of 1896, Dad, my brother Joe, some carpenters, and some of the neighbors began to hew timbers for the new barn. These timbers were from eight to ten inches square and from twenty-five to thirty feet in length and were all hand hewn. Men with regular axes would chip the side of a fallen tree and an expert broad-ax man would finish the work. When properly done, the finished timbers were perfectly square and almost as smooth as if they had been sawed at a sawmill. The barn ended up being seventy-five feet long and thirty-six feet wide and is still standing today (in 1964)! It required 144 pieces of these timbers to erect the frame. It was the largest barn in the neighborhood and Dad was quite proud of it. All these timbers were cut to size, mortised, and drilled in the barn-lot, and the whole frame was held together with one-inch wooden pegs. No nails were used in the frame. It took a lot of cooking to feed these hungry men when they came in from their work. Usually, three to four men stayed all night except on Saturday and Sunday. Mother and Mary had their hands full with three small children, one of which was a tiny baby, and all the housework to do.

Dad bought a large wooden pail with a lid and into this Mother packed enough eats for six men. They had a skillet and used it to heat the sausage or meat they had for the day. This way they lost little time for dinner. On Friday, Mother had a dish of hot noodles, or something similar, with sardines and Dad would come home and get it. This saved trying to reheat it, which is hard to do in the woods. On Saturday, Frank and I often brought them a hot dinner. I'll never forget one day on our way home, Frank was in the lead carrying the pail, while I was a few steps behind chewing on a ham bone. We were talking and laughing like boys will do, when a small piece of gristle from the bone lodged in my throat. Frank did not notice me, and I couldn't call for help. I thought for sure I would choke, but in laughing I had inhaled a deep breath and the sudden lung pressure forced the object from my throat. What a relief to be able to breathe again! I was sure scared for a few seconds.

Mr. Rothlei, the boss carpenter, was a very energetic man and would not stand for any fooling on the job. One windy day, while laying out timbers, Mr. Rothlei lost his hat denoting where the cuts were to be made for the mortising. The first time or two he reprieved it, but after that he let it lay and worked the rest of the day hatless. He said he didn't have time to chase after an old hat all day long. He always sat at one end of the table and if one of the other men sat in his place, he would make them move.

We had lots of fruit that summer, and Mother had done a lot of canning, so she had a good supply to draw from, along with a large quantity of dried apples and peaches. These she used in pies and we also ate them stewed. It took a lot of planning and cooking to keep a variety of food on the table for such a large crew of men. Some days there were a dozen or more men for lunch and supper. There were no supermarkets to go to in order to do any shopping. It was up to Mother to produce good meals from the things she had in the house. Knowing how to make different styles of dishes with the same article is the trick and Mother was well versed in that.

I don't remember how long it took to make the timbers and complete the barn, but it was quite hot when they finished so it must have been in June or July. The small timbers were all sawed at the mill, which meant that Dad and Joe had to cut the trees, make the logs, haul them to the mill, and then haul the lumber back home from there. It was quite a job for all concerned and a ten to twelve-hour day was not uncommon in those days. No coffee breaks either. The new barn was a big improvement through, and now Dad had ample room for his horses, farm implements, and also was able to store the wheat in the barn until it was ready for thrashing. No more stacking it outside. The barn also had a mechanical hayfork which made hay unloading not only much easier but faster too. It was a great improvement over the old method.

In the fall and winter of 1897, Dad, Joe, and a neighbor's boy cleared twelve acres of woods. All the timber for the new barn had been taken out of these woods, so only small trees remained. These had to be cut down and sawed into length to be rolled on piles and burned. The small sprouts were grubbed out by the roots, while the thorns and briers were cut with a scythe and piled up to be burned. This was exceedingly hard work, and a softy wouldn't have lasted long. The larger logs were rolled on piles with horses and chains since they were too heavy to be carried by men. The ground had to be completely free from all brush so it could be plowed in the spring. On Saturdays, Frank and I were allowed to come down and help, piling brush and old wood onto the fire. There was plenty to clean up before it was ready for a plow.

Following a plow was great fun, especially watching as it turned over the ground and covering the tall weeds. A heavy log-chain was used to accomplish this. It would drag the weeds down and the ground would fall on top of them. This would act as a mulch, and also prevent erosion.

A special kind of plow was used in plowing new ground. It took Joe twelve days to plow the twelve acres, with many whacks on the shins by roots. We had a team of bay mules and they were just what was needed on a job like this. That is the way our forefathers found this country and the way they brought it into fruition. Lots of sweat, hard work, and often disappointments when the crops failed due to weather conditions. All you can do is try again next year and hope for better luck.

THE DOCTOR & MEDICINES

Let me tell you what a country doctor was like in those days. If the doctor decided that he should see the patient before giving any medication, he would follow the caller to the home of the patient. After entering the sickroom, he would take his hat, usually a derby, also called a Stiff Katy, lay it on a chair, take a seat at the patient's bedside and begin his examination. First, he would call for a spoon and use the handle to depress the patient's tongue in order to examine their throat. Next, he took a temperature, felt the pulse, and go through the usual thumping procedure. Then, a few questions to the patient and the parents, if any, to familiarize himself with the patient's general condition. Now he was ready to prepare the medicine from the little black bag. If there were to be any tablets or pills, out came a little round box with lines on the lid where the directions were written. If powders were to be given, out would come a flat, flexible knife, then some paper, usually green or brown. If he didn't have any with him, he would ask for some. If nothing else was available, a newspaper was used. With the aid of a knife he would tear strips about two inches wide and three inches long. On each strip he would deposit a dose of powder and fold the paper so none could spill out. Next, he would call for a glass of water and a teaspoon. Into this he would mix some liquid medicine, sometimes only one or maybe two different kinds, depending on what he gave you or what it was for. After this he would give the mixture a stir. Then he would call Mother to give her instructions on how to administer the medicines, which usually went something like, "Give him one powder now and continue giving them one every three hours. In an hour give him a spoonful of the medicine in the glass and give that every four hours. About two o'clock, give him one of the pills and another at bedtime. Also give him a tablespoon of castor oil this afternoon." Mother would always repeat the instructions to make sure she had them right. Then the doctor would say, "Mr. Miller better come back in the morning and let me know how the boy is feeling." The doctor, Mother, and Dad would then have a little conference in the kitchen to go over the details of the illness, after which the doctor was off to the next call.

For all this, the doctor's charges were one dollar; two dollars if it was a night call. He seldom received cash but was paid later after the harvest was in or if some cash was obtained by selling a steer, some pigs, or some grain. Office calls were fifty cents, and this included some medicine. Sometimes the doctor would take eggs, firewood, home canned goods, etc. in place of money for his services.

The powder was placed on your tongue and you washed it down with a sip of water. I couldn't swallow pills, so they were crushed in a spoon and I took them like the powder. Liquid was easy but often very bitter. I took castor oil in black coffee as there was no orange juice to be had. Ugh, ugh! I still can taste it and see it floating on top of the coffee. How do I remember all these things? Because by the time I was nine years old I had taken more medicines than the average man takes in a lifetime, or that I, myself, have taken since then.

Mother had some home remedies that were used before a doctor was consulted. For coughs, there was elderberry jelly, honey and butter, or sugar with onion juice. Colds were cured with a bottle of C.C.C., otherwise known as "Certain-Chill-Cure", or there was "Dr. Mendenhall's Chill Cure". Both were miserable to take. A big dose of Epsom Salts first thing in the morning, was used as a laxative. It took a lot of courage to swallow that, but stern advice from Dad usually provided the courage. For stomach cramps, a few Hoffman Drops on a teaspoon of sugar settled the stomach. For diarrhea, Mother would put some whisky into a saucer, add a few tender peach leaves, and set it on fire. After it had burned a little while, she would put out the flame, and a teaspoon of this every hour would usually cure it. For ear-aches, sweet-oil and black pepper on a piece of cotton was inserted into the ear, while tooth-aches were soothed by placing a hot salt bag against the cheek and applying a little camphor-whisky directly on the offending tooth. Camphor-whisky was made by dissolving a piece of gum camphor in a bottle of good whisky. For frostbite, sprains, or aching muscles, a good rub with camphor-whiskey or Fox Liniment generally helped. If none of these remedies helped, you just suffered since aspirins were not known on the farm then. For cuts we had homemade salves. Nose bleeding was usually treated by sniffing salt water up your nose. For baby's colic there was Dr. Winslow's Soothing Syrup, and for constipation there was Castoria [castor oil]. There was also catnip, elderberry blossom, sage, and chamomile and peppermint teas. I don't remember what each was used for, but we always had them on hand in the green in summer and dried in the winter. Another remedy was a bottle of whisky with wild cherries in it. Again, I don't remember what it was used for.

With the nearest doctor three miles distant and no telephone to call him, people didn't run to the doctor for every little ache or pain that arose. Quite often these home remedies did relieve the aches and pains and when they didn't, you suffered until they were considered serious. Only then was a doctor consulted. There were several reasons for this. Most people were poor and put off calling a doctor as long as possible. Doctors were not trained like they are today, and they often made the wrong diagnosis, therefore being no help to the patient. Because of this, some people had no faith in them, but trying to avoid a doctor bill was often the main reason one wasn't called. Those days many people went for weeks without a penny in the house. I remember Dad saying that one time he was in Raben's Store with a terrible tooth ache. When Mr. Raben asked him why he didn't have the tooth extracted, Dad answered, *". . . because I haven't got the fifty cents to have it done."* Upon his reply, Mr. Raben gave him the half dollar and told him to go have it pulled out, which he did.

I wonder how our teenagers would fare today if they suddenly were confronted with situations like that. Laying all things aside, in many ways, people then were more contented and happier than they are today with all their modern conveniences.

SPRINGTIME

Around the middle of March, the weather would start to warm up, although we still had some cold days now and then. The buds would start to swell and the tulips, daffodils, crocuses, and hyacinth would poke their heads through the ground. When we first noticed them there was a race by us kids to Mother as each of us wanted to be the first to tell her. Then came the bleeding-hearts, lilies, peonies, and other perennials that we had in the garden. Mother would now make her hotbed to raise the cabbage, tomato, and sweet potato plants. Soon she would sow her lettuce and radish seeds, while the rest of the vegetable seeds were planted a little later, when the ground had warmed from the spring sun. Potatoes were planted and work started in the fields; oats sown, and corn planted. What an enchanting sight to see an orchard in full bloom, to listen to hundreds of bees gathering their honey, and to inhale the aroma from millions of blossoms.

March was also sassafras-teatime. Joe would go and dig up a bunch of sassafras roots, wash them real nice and clean, and cut them in small pieces as they would go into a tea pot. Twice a week, for about a month, we had sassafras-tea for supper instead of other teas or coffee. We all had to drink a cup of it. It wasn't bad tasting with a little sugar. It was supposed to thin your blood and tone you up for the warm weather soon to come. We used this in lieu of sulfur and molasses which some people used for the same purpose.

About this time, we moved the kitchen utensils out into the summer-kitchen and converted the winter-kitchen into a living room. The men folk helped with the stove and tables, and the rest was taken care of by Mother and us children.

After the kitchen was moved into the summer-kitchen, a rag carpet was laid down and the heating stove was moved from the bedroom to the winter kitchen, which now became the sitting room. This was just in case we should have a late cold spell. Some days were rather cool and damp, so a little fire in the stove made it more comfortable. One day, we kids were playing in this room. I had a long piece of string of which one end I had placed over the handle of the damper in the stovepipe. I was trying to put the other end of the string over the doorknob of the closet and make-believe it was a large belt running from an engine to a thrashing machine. The string didn't quite reach, and I was trying to stretch it a little, when suddenly, the stovepipe tumbled to the floor spilling soot all over the carpet. Immediately, the girls ran and told Mother and I got a good scolding, but I deserved it. It was a mess!

Many times, I had listened to a mud-wasp daubing mud on her nest on a rafter in the old simmer kitchen. It sounded almost like jiggling a bow on a violin string. Everywhere there was new life. Birds were building their nests and the mockingbird had returned to sing in the cedar tree or on top of the house.

Mother would lay away her shawl and put on her old sunbonnet and I would hunt up my straw hat with the tattered brim and chewing tobacco tags for ornaments. Supper was now eaten in daylight and the kerosene lamp disappeared from the table and was put away until fall. Mother was busy in the garden and ever so often I had to go and listen if the baby was crying. If so, I had to rock the cradle to try and out the baby back to sleep. There was a strong cord on the cradle and by leaving the door ajar we could sit on the outside in the other room and rock the baby. There were several deep grooves worn into the door jam from this cord sliding back and forth. At other times, Mother would send me to see what time it was so she wouldn't start supper late. I couldn't tell time yet, but I would tell her where the hands were and she would know by that. Even after almost seventy years I still can see her working in the garden.

What a joy it would be to relive those days, romping through the fields, hear the birds singing, and dig worms to go fishing. Have you ever listened to a meadowlark sing his SEOR-SEOR-SEOREE from the top of an old tree, or a cardinal from a clump of willows along a creek, with the water rippling over the gravel? Have you ever seen a squirrel scamper up a tree to his nest or watch the blackbirds follow a plow in spring and gobble up the worms and grubs from the fresh earth? Have you ever seen a song sparrow swing from a small bush in the fence row and listen to his song? It's an experience you never forget.

In back of our house stood a big apple tree and, after I was older, I use to make rope swings on which we children spent many a pleasant hour under that old tree. I had to make new ropes each year as the weather would weaken them and they were no longer safe to use. Why do so many people get bored with nature when God, in

His creation, has placed so many things for us to enjoy if we will only take the time to look about us.

Before I went to school I usually slept until about eight, when Mother would call me to get ready to take lunch to the men in the field by nine. I would get washed, have breakfast, and then start out with the lunch and a jug of fresh water. My sister, Rose, usually gave me assist with this task.

Every spring, all the fences around the house and the trees in the orchard were whitewashed. After I was about eight years old, I had to do my share of this work. This was usually done on a Saturday as we had no school and were at home. There were no Tom Sawyer's around eager to help and how the lime burned if you got some in the eyes. Those days on the farm taught you early to work and do what you were able to do in order to finish the many tasks that needed doing.

All seasons are beautiful in the country, but I believe spring outranks them all for beauty, fragrance, and invigoration of spirits, especially those of a little country boy. Those were the days when your heart was pure, your love deep, your trust absolute, and your cares small.

Everything has changed since then. Three years ago, when I visited my birthplace, there were a few apple trees left, the fences that I use to whitewash have long disappeared, the old summer-kitchen with its mud-wasps is gone and so are all the flowers Mother use to have in the garden. The creek has no more sand and gravel bottom, just yellow mud. The well house with its old oaken bucket, the swill barrel where I emptied many a crock of skim milk for the pigs, and the old hen-house where I picked up many an egg have all gone with the passing of time. Everything is changed but I still see it in my memory as it was long ago.

HOLYDAYS & HOLIDAYS

If we go by the calendar, we must start the holiday and holiday season with New Years. In the German neighborhood, this holiday was ushered in on New Year's Eve by shooting in the new year. A group of men would go from farm to farm and fire a volley of shots, after which they were welcomed into the house for refreshments, some of which was hard cider. They never stopped at our house since Dad made it known that they were not welcomed. Dad had several good reasons for this. We all know that a loaded gun can be dangerous in the hands of a sober person, but when it is carried by a person under the influence of strong drink, it is doubly dangerous. Once, at my Uncles house, a man laid a full powder horn in a pail of hot ashes. My uncle discovered it in time to remove it before it exploded. The guns used were mostly old muzzle-loaders which were loaded by hand, and a man with too much to drink could easily overload a gun and cause it to explode. I personally knew three men with arm stubs caused by exploding guns, which some happened while hunting. Another reason my Dad never allowed these men in the house was that often the roads were a sea of mud and the house would look like a pig sty after the men had gone. Now you can understand why New Year's shooting was not welcomed at our house.

Our first Holyday was February 2, or Candlemas Day. Some of us always attended mass. I remember once when my sister Mary and I went. It was near zero and we left early enough to go to confession before mass and receive communion. I forgot to wear my ear cap and soon my ears began to smart from the cold. By the time we reached the church my left ear was frozen stiff. When it warmed up it began to swell and by the time mass was over it was twice it's normal size. It took weeks to get it back to normal again and was so tender that I had to keep it covered if it was the least bit chilly.

Valentine's Day was not celebrated nor was Mardi Gras. Sometimes, Mother would make a batch of fried cakes (doughnuts to you) but that was all.

Decoration Day was just another day. Once some Civil War Vets had a memorial service at the Lutheran Cemetery which was about one mile from our house, but that is the only one I can recall.

The Fourth of July was usually celebrated with a picnic at Haines Grove and was given by the St. Wendel Band, if there was a band. Otherwise there was no celebration close by. If a picnic was held, Dad would give me a quarter and I was permitted to go but I had to be home before sundown. Bartel Bender, at St. Joe's, always had a picnic, but that was eight miles away and too far for us to go. One Fourth of July I'll never forget, I was about eleven years old and I had the worst case of measles you ever want to see. While the rest of the family were celebrating at our neighbors with beer, lemonade, ice cream, and other good eats, I was at home in bed with a woolen blanket up to my chin with the temperature one hundred degrees in the shade, bemoaning my dilemma. Such is life!

Usually on a Sunday afternoon, the St. Wendel Band would assemble and give a sort of concert for the people who had come for church vespers. It was also a practice session, and the people enjoyed the music. Father Pfeiffer was a great man for show. When we had a procession to the cemetery, like on the Holyday of Corpus Christi, he would ask the band to take part and play a few pieces of sacred music, which they had learned. On Christmas and Easter, they were in the choir loft and played during the Offertory and after Mass. Some people thought the band was out of place at church, but Father was the boss, so we had band music at Mass.

During Lent we had the Stations of the Cross on Wednesdays and Fridays, with benediction added on Friday. Some of the adults always tried to go both days, work and weather permitting. Palm Sunday was celebrated with a procession on the cemetery, with everyone carrying a small cedar branch. We had no palms to carry.

Easter, Pentecost, and Christmas were the main Holydays. The finest vestments were used, the alters were aglow with candles and artificial flowers, the singing was beautiful, and twelve altar boys were serving. Six dressed in white and six in red cassocks.

On Holy Saturday we made the Easter-nests for the bunny to lay his eggs in. We drove sticks in a circle, filled it with grass to make it soft for the bunny to sit on, and placed a little handful of clover in front of the nest so he could eat while laying the eggs. Oh, the beauty of a small child's trust and beliefs. When the nests were all finished, we showed them to Mother and pointed out to whom each nest belonged. The next morning, we all had our eggs. One year, for some reason, Mother didn't have any eggs for us and what a disappointment that was. We hunted all over, thinking that the bunny might have hid them among the flowers, but no eggs were to be found anywhere.

As soon as we were old enough to talk, Mother started to teach us our prayers. This she did in the morning while she was making the beds in her bedroom. We had to kneel down and repeat after her some short prayers, until we were older. Then, we were taught the Our Father, Hail Mary, Apostles Creed, the Acts of Faith, Hope, and Charity, and the Act of Contrition. By the time we started school we knew all these prayers and could recite them with ease, whenever Sister asked us to do so. We learned the names of the Angels by saying the Angel prayers at Meals. We said the Our Father and Hail Mary before each meal, and the Angels afterwards. No one ate or left the table until these prayers were said, and they were said regardless of who might be having a meal with us.

Night prayers were also said every night. These consisted of two decades of the rosary one night, and three decades the next night. We also said the Litany of Our Blessed Mother and one Our Farther and Hail Mary for the Poor Souls. One night, while we were saying our prayers, a little mouse came out of the closet under the stairs, became confused, and ran up Frank's pant leg. He caught the little thing and accidentally squeezed it to death. On another occasion, we were all kneeling when my little brother, who was about three years old, and was sitting in his highchair, suddenly started to cry loudly. When Mother asked why he was crying, he said there was a big snake hanging on the towel rack. The towel rack was a steel rod about 3/8 inches thick with a knob on one end. Mother used it to poke the fire when it didn't burn good. Well, none of us saw anything. We all wondered what it could have been that he saw, as the rod was completely empty. He must have seen something to bring on such a spell. We never found out, nor did we ever have a reoccurrence.

When I was about ten years old, I received my parent's permission to become an altar boy. First, I had to learn the Latin prayers, then I was used as an extra at high-Mass when there were four altar boys. The two leaders did all the serving, while we just answered the responses. After about three months, I served my first Mass as a leader. My cousin and I served the eight o'clock low-

Mass on Christmas Day. We completed the Mass without making a mistake. Father Pfeiffer was very strict, so we tried very hard to do everything right. One Corpus Christi Sunday, I was elected to carry the large Missal from which Father read a gospel at each altar. The gospel at the first altar was very long and went down to the bottom of the page. When Father moved my fingers so he could see the print, I almost dropped the book. I was sweating and was glad when he finished. I guess Father thought so too, as we had a much lighter book the next year. On feast days like this, there were always twelve altarboys; six in red and six in white. When we celebrated the Golden Anniversary of the church in 1903, four altar boys (the leaders) were dressed in golden cassocks, while the rest were in red and white. The church is still standing after giving one hundred and eleven years of service and is used every day.

While Father was strict, he was also very good to us. Every morning after Mass, he gave each of us a piece of candy. On Christmas, each of us servers received a bag of candy, nuts, and an orange. On Easter Sunday, we received a bag containing three Easter eggs.

Father Pfeiffer also inaugurated the custom for us to get an offering from the bride and groom and a wedding. He did this by giving us his cincture with which we blocked the back door of the church until we received a donation. I remember one couple who were not blessed with riches. When we stepped across the open doorway, the groom reached into his pocket and came up with four nickels, gave each of us one, and said, "Here is your chunk. What a chunk!" We understood what he meant and were satisfied with it. One dollar was the most we ever received at one wedding. All the money we received was turned in to Sister until the end of the school year, when she divided it amongst all the altar boys. If you served every time you were scheduled, you received more, as Sister penalized those who missed the schedule. The boys who served every morning during vacation received something extra for their service. One year, I received over a dollar for my share. It doesn't sound like much, but a dollar then was equal to ten dollars today.

In the winter, when our shoes were often too muddy to go into the sanctuary, we changed into low cuts. I didn't have any of my own, but the other boys who had some left them in back of the altar and permitted me to use them.

It was a wonderful experience to serve at the altar and be so close to God. Once, I wished to become a priest and prayed to God for guidance, but I guess I was destined to marry. Now it is my hope that our son, James, will, with God's grace, fill that place. Four more years will tell. *(Yes, the author's son, James R. Miller, was ordained a priest on June 1, 1968.)*

Every year, on or about October 20, Forty Hour Devotion started. October 20 is the Feast of St. Wendel. There is a Mass in the morning and an evening service at 7:30, consisting of rosary, sermon, and benediction. After this, confession was heard. The school children had hours of adoration until about four o'clock in the afternoon when we went home. Father Francis was the speaker in the evening, in German of course. The third day was the closing, which concluded with a procession around the cemetery. Once in a while I was allowed to go along to the evening services. That was quite a thrill to drive home in the dark. It didn't take much to thrill us kids.

Once, our Bishop came from Indianapolis for the Confirmation of a large class during the Forty Hours Devotion. He was met at the station by a mounted parade, and my Dad was the parade marshal. He polished the riding bridle, bought two brass buttons for the bridle's head band, and gilded the bit and buckles with gold paint. He also bought a woolen saddle blanket that was dark green with gold edging and a gold star in the corner on each side. Old Dan, the horse, was given a slick grooming and was all quite ritzy. After all, the Bishop didn't come to St. Wendel every year so this had to be good. After the parade, the saddle and blanket hung in the granary. The mice ate a large hole in the blanket and used it to line their nests for their babies. I bet they were nice and warm. We seldom went anywhere on horseback and the blanket wasn't used much, so the hole wasn't noticed until it was too late.

Labor Day and Thanksgiving were not celebrated at our house, and Christmas was the last Holyday of the year. The first signs of Christmas appeared when the two general stores in St. Wendel placed their toys in the windows. On the way home from school we would stand outside with our little noses pressed against the window admiring the things we saw. The toys were very simple; a few carts with a pony, a wind-up toy or two, some blocks, books, drums, dishes, a jack-in-the-box, and a few dolls. The whole window full of toys wasn't worth more than twenty-five dollars. We would go from one store to the other, talking about what we expected Krist-Kindle (Christ-Child) to bring us. Old Santa Claus didn't bring the presents down there. He meted out the punishments to bad children and always carried a stick. Looking through the glass was, for most of us, as close as we came to any store toys. I myself never had a store toy in all my life. If you had a real good uncle or godfather and luck was with you, you might get a store toy, as most parents didn't have any money to buy them. The first couple of days we were a little late coming home from school as we would look until we had seen everything. Some kids with extra nerve would go inside so they could see better. My poor Mother, how her heart must have ached when we came home and told her all about what we had seen and what we would like to have for Christmas, knowing that our dreams would not be fulfilled, as she didn't have the money to buy us toys.

While I was still small, on Christmas Eve, after the dishes were done, Mary would set the table for breakfast by turning the plates upside down. Along each plate was a slip of paper with the name of the person that sat at this place. This would enable Krist-Kindle to know where to place each present. These slips were made by cutting off the white margin on the newspaper above the printed material. As usual, the night prayers were said and all retired, hoping we would receive the presents we asked for. The sandman seemed never to come that night. About three o'clock the next morning, some of the adults would get up to go to five o'clock Mass. After I started going to school, I usually went along too. Due to the condition of the roads we usually walked to Mass. This was one of the few mornings of the year when one wake-up call found me jumping out of bed in a hurry! We ate little breakfast as we were too excited over the presents we had received. These usually were some type of clothing, gloves, stockings, handkerchiefs, some dolls for the girls, and maybe a harmonica or jack-knife for Frank and me. Joe and Mary would get some kind of clothing or yard goods for shirts or a dress or something similar. How easy it would be today to do your Christmas shopping if this custom still existed, instead of all those expensive things people go in debt for today.

About 3:45 we left for church as we had about one hour to walk. While women and children went into church to keep warm, the men folk stopped off at the saloon for a warm-up nip or two. It was custom for the barkeep to present each customer with a small bottle of whisky as a Christmas present. I got my first one when I was about twenty years old.

The church was dimly lit with kerosene lamps. These were fastened to the pillars and didn't give much light, but that was all they had at in 1898. How our eyes would open when we saw the altars all decorated with the flowers and candles. There was no crib set then, but years later, the priest got one. It was about half-life size, complete with a stable.

When we first got there, the church was quite empty, but by Mass time it was full. The school children all sat in the choir loft and, about five minutes before Mass started, sang a beautiful Christmas hymn. There was a Low Mass at eight o'clock and another High Mass at ten. Sometimes I was allowed to remain for all three Masses. Everyone you met would say, "Christmas Gift!", which was sort of asking for something, like a piece of candy. Generally, the reply would be, "You get nothing!", unless the person did have some candy and was willing to part with a piece. At three in the afternoon we had Vespers, or prayers, and after I reached my teens, I usually went, weather permitting. I loved the beautiful singing by our choir.

Christmas dinner was the same as any Sunday dinner. Fresh pork with sauerkraut, mashed potatoes with the trimmings, plus a three-layer cake; one white, one yellow, and one pink with hard icing dotted with small pieces of candy.

While I was still small, Christmas was just about over after the dishes were washed as eight o'clock was bedtime. After I was older and had a little spending money, Frank and I would buy a few firecrackers and roman candles and these we shot off after it got dark. This event ended Christmas day for another year. It wasn't much but I believe we had more fun and a lot deeper religious fervor than the people have today.

I can remember having only two Christmas trees, as evergreens were very scarce in our part of the country. I was about eleven years old when we had the first one. It was set up in Grandma's room with the candles tied to the bows. After saying the rosary, Dad went in by the side door, lit all the candles, and set off the alarm on the old clock on the bureau. This was the signal for Mother to bring us in the room. We shook like an aspen from the excitement, as well as the cold, as there was no fire in the room. Dad would leave by the side door, dragging a heavy log across the back porch, scaring us into believing the Old Santa was leaving with his stick.

Christmas was the only time of the year when oranges could be bought in the country, so we always got an orange with our candy and nuts. Mother distributed these goodies and we all received the same. Children believed in the Krist-Kindle until they were ten or eleven years old and were sure all the gifts were brought by It. Their eyes would light up like stars when they entered the room and saw their gifts. Children would have a lot more fun at Christmas time if they still held this child-like trust and expectation we had when I was a child at Christmas. Now, a child must know and have everything and express himself to the point of telling Santa Claus to go to hell if he isn't satisfied with his gift!

Yes, the world has changed, but for a lot of innocent fun and enjoyment give me the old days when children respected their adults and were thankful for any gift or favor received.

CHORES

Until I was about seven years old there wasn't much work, I could help with except rock the baby and pick up a little around the house, especially in the winter. After I was a year or two older I helped a lot by making the upstairs beds, dusting the furniture, carrying the skim milk from the cellar, turning the butter churn, picking up plums and apples that had fallen from the trees during the night, gathering the ripe tomatoes, drying the dishes, and helping in the garden. There was also kindling wood to cut, grass to mow, the wood-box to be filled, eggs to hunt, and water to pump for the cattle and pigs. In hot weather, Mother let the fire go out in the cook stove, so about 4:30 in the afternoon I use to restart it so she could cook supper.

During wheat harvest I carried bundles together so Joe and Frank could shock them, which was stacking the sheaves of grain upright in the field to dry. One year, our wheat had grown very tall, so I had to follow the binder all day and pull the bundles from the machine so they would not be all tied together. By night I had walked many a mile. When they were cultivating corn, I followed the plow cutting out the weeds around the stumps or those missed by the cultivator. During the first plowing I also had to plant pumpkin seeds every fifth row and about twenty feet apart. This was done on Saturday when I was home from school.

Sometimes I helped operate the hand powered washing machine or turn the wringer to wring out the clothes. Mother boiled all the white and colored clothes, and all were washed twice, with a water change between each washing. Before we had the cistern, a receptacle for holding water, Mother, Mary, and Joe would carry the water for washing from a spring about two blocks from the house. This they did by carrying the wash boiler between them and a pail in the other hand. Our well water was too hard for washing. If it rained, they would catch water from the roof in rain barrel and some tugs to wash with. Every Monday was wash day, unless it was pouring rain, and every Tuesday was ironing day. An average wash day consisted of the equivalent of six modern large loads of clothes. Mother used homemade soap made from lye and grease and cooked in a big iron kettle. Mary did most of the ironing, and everything had to be ironed, even the sheets and pillowcases. Mother would iron dad's white shirt as that was a special shirt and had to be ironed just right. The old-fashioned cast iron was used with its iron handle. Mary had to use a pad to protect her hands but occasionally burned them anyway. The iron was heated on the cook stove, so a hot fire was needed, and in hot weather this added to the tiresome job and heat of the day.

I used to make the upstairs beds. This was quite a job as the featherbed was removed so we could get to the straw-sack, as we called it. This was made from heavy ticking and was filled with corn husks instead of straw. These husks were all fluffed up and evened out so the bed was uniform. Then, the feather bed was put back and the sheet was tucked in all around. This was followed by an all wool blanket, two quilts, and a comforter, all of which were tucked in well at the foot of the bed. This was done in the winter only, while only a sheet and one quilt was used in the summer.

We had quite a few rail fences then, and these were often moved so we could change the cattle from one field to another. This was a disagreeable job, especially in windy weather, as the dirt from the rails would blow into your eyes and down your neck.

Dad always cut and split enough wood for the stoves in winter to use all year and this had to be piled in rows. I piled wood many times on a Saturday when I had other things in mind, but orders were orders and I obeyed them or else.

Shining the shoes for Sunday was a job for every Saturday, and in the winter, this was a real job since they were often quite muddy. Only Mother and Mary had rubbers for their shoes, so the men's and children's shoes were usually plenty muddy, though they tried to clean them the best they could. I used Mason's Water-Solvent Polish, so if it was dry a little spit would solve the problem. Keeping the ash pit on the stove clean was also one of my jobs.

In the fall, after the pumpkins were ripe, I would break a bunch by throwing them on the ground and feed them to the pigs. I had to save the seeds, wash them out, and spread them on boards to dry. After they had all been dried, Dad took them to town where he received about three cents a pound for them. This money was to be Frank's spending money. Speaking of pigs, I was quite a hog caller and could raise them from the farthest corner of the farm!

Once we had a mother pig with six little ones. The mother died and, as the little ones were too small to live without her, we fed them milk with nipple bottles. At first, we had them in a box. Then, when they were larger, we kept them in a pen, until they were large enough to run with the older pigs. They were so cute and when feeding time came, they all squealed at once. It took some time to feed them as we had to hold the bottle for them.

I learned to milk cows when I was about ten, and from then I usually helped with the milking in the evening. In early Spring, when the grass was nice and green along the road, but the pasture was still too soft for the cattle to be on, Frank and I would take them out on the road to graze. We were about a quarter mile apart from each other and that gave them plenty of room to graze in. We watched them for about three hours and then brought them back in the lot.

One job I hated was to pick spring chickens. Shortly after dinner on a Saturday, we had to help Mother catch two. Sometimes it was quite a job to corner them. After we caught them, they were put in a coup so they would recover from their running. Mother would cut their heads off and scald them. We kids had to pick them clean, and I mean clean! After that, Mother took care of the rest. The next day, we had either fried or roast chicken, or chicken and dumplings. No matter which, it was always a wonderful, tasty dinner, Yum, yum!

All the boys in my school room said they were going fishing on Easter Monday and I always had the urge too, but I usually had some chores to do instead and so I didn't go. How I hated to pick potato bugs, but like it or not, I picked them just the same. Later on, we found out how to poison them by mixing Paris-Green with wood ashes and sifting this on the plants early in the morning while they were still wet with dew. That ended the bug picking job and was much more satisfactory as it really got them all.

Whenever I hunted the eggs, I used an old black felt hat that I always wore on Saturday or after I came home from school. It would hold about two dozen eggs. It was actually Frank's hat that he wore with his First Communion suit. When it got dirty on the inside, I simply reversed it and all was okay, sort of a dispy-doodle trick. I bet my Mother loved me when she saw me with this hat on, along with a dirty face, stockings hanging down to the shoe tops, and an innocent grin on my face like a kitten that just finished lapping up a dish of milk. No wonder the expression, "A face only a mother could love!"

I had to get up early and cut off all the sweet potato vines so the frost wouldn't follow the vines to the roots and turn the potatoes black. This had to be done before the frost melted, so I had to start early as we had several rows of them.

After the new barn was built, hauling in the wheat became quite a job. Joe and Frank did the hauling, while Dad, Mother, and us kids did the unloading. This way we could haul with two wagons and do the job in half the time. Poor Mother had the hardest job of all as she would pick up every bundle and place it just so. She did this until she was fifty years old, and many times she bumped her head on the big beams. We kids would place the bundles as near as we could, but she would place all of them in perfect alignment to suit her. There was so much work on the farm in those days than there is today, and so much of it had to be done by hand, much more than most people can imagine. Help was hard to get and most people didn't have the money to hire help, even if it had been available. I once heard Mother say that when she and Dad first got married, she worked in the field during harvest time until it was time to nurse the baby. She would go home and feed the baby and then go back again to the field. This she did both in the morning and afternoon until supper time, after which, she did the housework that the schoolgirl they had as a helper wasn't able to do. Those days, a schoolgirl, twelve or thirteen years old, would work for a farm family for about seventy-five cents a week. She would mind the babies, peel the potatoes, make the beds, wash the dishes, and do whatever jobs there were that she was able to do.

The people were poor and by working this way they were, with a little luck, able to become established and gradually build a debt-free home life and raise their families. Too bad some of these mothers who become bored with their city life, with all its conveniences, can't be forced to undergo a life like my Mother had for just a couple weeks. It might wake them up and make them realize what their fore-fathers and mothers went through to build this country for them and make all the things they have to enjoy possible. I am sure many of them would be a lot better off if they kept themselves busy.

Let me regress for a moment and say a few words in regards to all of us working as we did. Wheat was selling at fifty cents a bushel, corn at twenty-five cents a bushel, eggs at ten cents a dozen, butter at twelve cents a pound, and clover hay for one dollar a load that all two horses could pull. One year, my Dad gave it away for free because he had no sale for it. Pigs were selling for four cents a pound, and a four-week old calf for five dollars. These were the things a farmer depended on for his income and at these prices, his income was very limited and therefore he had no money with which to hire help. This is why we all did our share to help and get the work done. No one was ever overworked. Besides, work does not kill anyone, if done in an orderly, sensible manner.

A TYPICAL DAY

During the winter, the day started about six in the morning, when Dad, Mother, and we children would get up so we would leave in time to be at eight o'clock Mass. Dad started the fire in the cook stove and then went to the barn to do the feeding, while Mother got us out of bed and prepared breakfast. The breakfast menu varied from day to day; bacon and eggs, fried potatoes with cottage cheese, sausage and cheese, and maybe pancakes. Mother made five different kinds of pancakes along with French toast. In the winter, we had buckwheat pancakes about twice a week. Of course, bread and butter was also on the breakfast table. In the summer, when there was a lot more work to be done, we rose at five in the morning. Because of the flies, the milking had to be done early as the cows would not stand still once the flies started biting.

The men folk were in the fields shortly after sun-up, and Mother and Mary went on with their housework. Much of this depended on the time of the year. During the summer, there was much work in the garden and they also helped in the fields, especially during hay and wheat harvest. Then, all the canning had to be done as the fruit ripened. During the winter, the sewing was done, as was the making of quilts and comforters.

In the summer, we had lunch at nine o'clock in the morning. If the men were working close to the house they came in for lunch, otherwise, we kids brought it to them. At eleven-thirty the dinner bell was rung and about noon we ate dinner. At one-thirty they went back to the field until four-thirty and ate supper at five o'clock. After supper it was back to the field until sun-down. Back then, dinner and supper were two separate meals, not like today.

When we kids were old enough we would do some of the chores like carrying straw into the stable to bed down the horses, throw down some hay from the loft, and put the corn in the feed-box. When I was about ten years old, I helped with the milking. Actually, taking care of the milk was the last job of the day. It was all strained into one-gallon crocks and carried into the cellar. Here it sat for three days after which the cream was skimmed off and the milk was poured into the swill barrel and fed to the pigs, along with whatever other waste we had. Strange as it may seem, we children drank very little milk. Raw milk from the cow doesn't taste as good as the milk we drink here in the city. The taste of milk is affected by the feed the cow eats. If they were on clover pastures, the milk didn't taste very good, and after the weeds came up the milk tasted bitter. Some nights we would mix some with water as this would alter the taste and we would have a drink, but not every night.

Bread was baked twice a week, usually on Wednesday and Saturday. On Saturday, Mother usually would bake seven loaves of bread, six coffee cakes, a pan of buns for Sunday breakfast, and sometimes a pound cake.

In the winter the kitchen floor had to be scrubbed every Saturday afternoon. The boards were six inches wide and a scrub brush was used with a good supply of home-made soap. I did this one winter when Mary was working in town for a Mrs. Salem. About every two weeks the kitchen flatware and the brass hoops on the cedar water pail were polished with brick dust. There were no fancy cleaners or scouring powders at that time. We made the brick dust by pounding pieces of soft brick until it was like fine powder. The stone step at the porch had two cup-like holes which were ideal for this job.

We always ate three full meals a day, which meant cooking a meal three times a day! When school was in season, we did our homework after supper, and about seven-thirty in the evening, Dad was ready for night prayers. By eight o'clock we were all ready for bed, unless one of the neighbors dropped in and stayed awhile. Dad claimed that three hours of sleep before midnight were more beneficial than five hours of sleep after midnight, so we all went to bed early, and no talking in bed!

A TRIP TO TOWN

Dad traveled to Evansville about every four weeks. Grandpa, my two uncles, and my Dad took turns so at least one of them went every week. We exchanged all our butter, eggs, and produce for groceries at Mrs. Cooper's, so seldom was there any money involved. We traded there for twenty-four years. After Grandpa died and one uncle quit farming, it became necessary for Dad to go every two weeks, so he found a market closer to home and we seldom went to Evansville anymore.

Sometimes, when Dad went to town, he did not stop for a hot dinner. He would buy a loaf of rye bread and a piece of bologna sausage and eat a lunch on the way home. There was always some left over which he brought home for us kids. Boy, was that a treat! Once in a while, he would buy a dozen bananas for fifteen cents, or a pack of gum. We sure appreciated that. When you realize that Dad went to town once a month, and many times brought us nothing, you can understand why we were so elated when he brought us a little treat.

After I was about ten years old, I was allowed to go along on one trip each year during vacation. Boy was that a thrill! It was one of those days when it only took one call to get me out of bed. Dad usually took a load of wheat and we had all dirt roads which were quite hilly. This meant slow driving, so to keep the butter from getting too soft from the heat, we left real early. I remember once, we were halfway to town by the time the sun rose. Dad used to tell me that if the first person we saw was young, we would get good prices for our produce. If it was an old lady, the contrary would be the case. This was just an old German saying through, and we didn't put any stock in it.

It was too bad we only had two eyes, as there was so much to see. Street cars, trains, and maybe even a fire engine if we were lucky. There were also tall buildings, four stories high! If Dad had any business on Water Street, we even saw the Ohio River, which is quite wide there. Dad didn't make any special effort to show us any special scenery, but there was so much to see just in the places we did go. If we drove on the street with a streetcar coming behind us. the motorman would clank his bell. It would scare the horses and it seemed to us that he did more clanking than necessary, probably just to see the horses act up. Those days, a farmer was considered a rube or yokel and everybody poked fun at them.

It was amusing to me to read the signs in town. Some were large billboards while others were tacked on fences, trees, or wherever they found space to put them. I remember seeing "Sherman-Williams Paint Covers the Earth", and "Dr. Bell's Pine-Tar and Honey Cough-Syrup". There were many different brands of chewing and smoking tobacco advertised, such as "Dukes Mixture", "Bull-Durham Smoking Tobacco", "Black Diamond", La Fendrick", "Cinco Cigars", and others. There was also "Theo. E. Rechting Lumber Company" at 7th and Ingle Street's, and "Selz Shoes," which showed two laughing feet with the title, "Make your feet glad!". I remember seeing a billboard for "Mica Axle Grease", which was a Standard Oil product, which showed two loaded wagons being pulled by two teams of horses. The team pulling the wagon, greased with Mica Axle Grease, ambled along as though the wagons were empty, while the team pulling the other wagon, greased with a competitive brand, were struggling as though they were trying to move a mountain. Laughable? Yes, but times haven't changed.

There were beer signs advertising all three brewery's that were around at that time. The Washburn and Crosby Flour sign had a slogan that read, "Eventually . . . why not now?" This had me confused for a long time as I didn't know the meaning of the word "eventually". Washburn and Crosby are now General Mills and Betty Crocker. The sticker of them all was the sign for "Pond's Extract". Extract, to me, meant to pull out, like extracting a tooth, and a pond was a water hole for pigs to wallow in, so how could you extract that? "Eventually" and "extract" were pretty big words for a ten-year-old kid that talked nothing but German all year round. Maybe I was just a little ignorant too, but I did get their meaning later on.

Dad put up the team in a wagon-yard and fed them with some feed that we had brought along. There was a dining room at the yard, so we always ate a hot dinner. After dinner, Dad did what shopping there was to do, and about two o'clock we started back for home.

Just outside of the city limits was a big hill named Babytown Hill, after the little village that was there. From the top of this hill you could see the whole town of Evansville with its smoking factory chimneys. Here, we kids took another good look at the city, for it would be another year before we would see it again.

About 1903, Dad decided that we needed a new rig to go to church with, as the old express was getting pretty shabby. One day, he and I went to town and, after dinner, went to Rosenberger Klein and Company to see what they had in the line of new rigs. One vehicle was a surrey with a fringe on top (just like the song says) and it was a beauty. It was a James & Meyer product, with a black body and brewster-green gear, but there was the price. After some haggling, Dad and the salespeople came to an agreement and we bought it. Boy, did we kids think we were somebody now! There was nothing like it in all of St. Wendel. It was used only when the roads were in good condition so that no mud would get on it. If we were caught in a shower, it had to be washed the next day for sure. After all, it cost $115 and had to look the part. Wow!

Automobiles did not appear in that area until about 1910 when Mr. Chute, the E. & T. H. Station Master in Poseyville bought a little buggy type of car with the motor in back of the seat and a tiller for steering. A little later, Mr. Seiler, the livery-barn man, bought a Brush Runabout with the wooden front axle. About 1911, the two Kale boys, who were farmers, bought an Acme Five passenger touring car. They were followed by Mr. Taylor, the barber, and Mr. Nix, the blacksmith. Both also bought Acme touring cars, while Mr. Bozeman, the banker, bought a Marmon. A short time later, a Mr. Knowles opened an Overland dealership in Cynthiana, so farmers started to drive Overlands, and the race was on! Fords came in a little later, after I left the farm in February of 1912, when I was twenty-two years old.

SUMMERTIME

Although summer doesn't officially start until June 21, it was always warm enough in May to go barefoot, which we often did on our way home from school. We did this without our parents' consent, and then put the shoes back on when we got close to home. How we went all summer without getting our feet all cut up, I don't know. Oh, we would get a cut once in a while, but nothing serious. If we worked in the field, we wore an old pair of shoes without stockings.

About the middle of June, the harvest season would begin with the cutting of the clover hay. The wheat came next, and then the Timothy hay was cut. Before we had the new barn, all the hay was unloaded by hand and this was a slow and hot job. Joe would pitch it into the mow and Dad and Mother would throw it back, while Frank and I would trample on it. The next, and one of the hardest jobs, was the hauling of the manure from the barn-lot out into the fields. Sometimes we would have a neighbor boy to help with this job, if Dad could get one. It took about one week to do this job. By now we were running barefoot all day, and by nightfall our feet were completely black. It was lots of fun to wade in the water washing our feet, and after a good rain when everything looked so nice and green and smelled so fresh.

The first ripe fruit were always the cherries. These came in about the third week in May, followed by the plums, raspberries, gooseberries, blackberries, and every other year, the apples. The apple tree had fruit only one year out of two. Peaches and grapes came in a little later. I still can see the apples and peaches drying on long boards in the hot sun. Apples were peeled and sliced about one-half inch thick, while peaches were not peeled at all. If they were free of pits or stones, they were cut in half and dried that way. Clingstones were out in bread pans and placed in the oven for a few minutes until they started to wrinkle, and then placed on the boards where they finished drying until they looked like a piece of dry bark. When they were cooked, they would return to their original size.

On real hot days, as you looked across the fields, you could see the heat shimmer as though it came from an underground furnace. I enjoyed lying in the shade of a tree to watch the big white clouds standing in the sky like mountains, changing their forms as they went rolling along. I would watch a cloud shadow as it raced down a hill over the fence, across a little dell, and up the hill on the other side. Often, on hot days, while walking along the road or in a field, I would watch a shadow approach, and I would stand still until it reached me to enjoy the shade while it lasted. This, of course, depended on the size and speed of the cloud. What fun it would be to be a small boy again for a few weeks and relive some of these memories.

We raised our navy beans by planting them in with the corn. The picking was done when the temperature was around one hundred degrees in the shade. You crept along on your knees from plant to plant, dragging a grain bag into which you put the beans. With the sweat running down your face and the dry corn leaves cutting your neck, this was a pretty tough job for a kid, and a lot tougher than peddling papers or mowing a lawn like today.

Wheat thrashing was done in August. About a dozen farmers banded together, which was known as a company, to help each other. That was always a big day for us kids with lots of good eats. Mother usually had roast beef, boiled ham, and all the trimmings to make it a real meal. One thing we always had as prune pie and sugared donuts. If we thrashed on a Friday, we had both meat and sardines, as some of the men were not Catholic. In those days, Catholics didn't eat meat on Friday through the whole year, and not just during Lent like today. Once, because of rain, we were not able to trash on a Thursday, so we thrashed the next day. Mother was not prepared for a Friday meal, so she sent me to St. Wendel to get some sardines. I wore a new pair of all wool pants without a pair of underwear, or drawers as they were called then. By the time I came home my legs were almost raw. Those pants were like sandpaper!

When I was a wee shaver, I was very scared of the thrasher engine whistle and would crawl under the bed when the thrasher pulled into our yard. I can still recall those old separators, as thrashing machines were called then. They had neither blowers for blowing the straw on a pile in the lot, or a self-feeder to feed the bundles of grain into the machine. This was done by one man and the straw was stacked by several men with forks. An elevator-like conveyor carried it up on the pile, but it had to be properly stacked so there would be enough room in the lot to contain it all.

Along with all the hot jobs there were also pleasant times, like cutting a big juicy watermelon, enjoying a glass of Mother's lemonade, or a piece of fresh bread with jelly, preserves, or apple butter spread on it. Mother had a one quart earthen-ware cream pitcher. This she filled every morning and sat on the rear of the stove. This would heat the milk and sort of pasteurize it. Sometimes I would take the cream that gathered on top of this milk and put it on my bread and preserves. That's good eating and better than whipped cream.

At night in the summertime, the lightening bugs were out by the thousands. I have never seen them so numerous as down there. All night long you would hear the insects chirp, the Katy-Dids with their rasping "kat-kat", and the screech owls in the apple tree just outside our bedroom window. I must tell you a little incident about one of these little creatures. We had just gone to bed when one of these owls started screeching, just outside the window. This annoyed Joe and he went to the window trying desperately to shoo it away. Well, Mr. Owl would not be shooed, so Joe got up, went outside, and threw an old bottle up into the tree. This quieted the owl and Joe came upstairs satisfied that all was well. He had barely laid down when Mr. Owl started screeching again. By now Joe was all shook up and, getting up, he got the shotgun and fired a shot into the tree. This started me laughing. Joe put the shotgun away and was hardly in bed again when that darn owl started merrily screeching as before! Joe finally gave up and went to sleep.

One morning, Dad saw a large horn owl sitting on the roof of the old barn and shot it. He then set the bird on the side of the old stable. When Rose and I got up, Dad told us about it and we darted out in our underwear to see it. Mother chased us back in the house as she didn't approve of us running around in the yard in such clothes. How times have changed!

One thing I feared in the summer were the thunderstorms we had. The lightening would flash almost continuously, and the thunderclaps were deafening at times. We saw three barns burn in one night, all struck by lightning during a single storm.

There was a large oak tree in our field just about mid-way between our house and our neighbors. Here we kids played every Sunday afternoon and in this way, learned to speak the English language. These children knew no German and we didn't know any English. At first, it was a little tough going, but we soon learned to understand each other. They learned a little German and we learned a lot of English.

At that time there were no barbers in St. Wendel, and with the nearest one about seven miles distant, Dad went to a neighbor for his haircuts, usually on a Sunday afternoon. Dad took care of our hair himself. Since he didn't like the job of cutting our hair, he cut them plenty short so we wouldn't need another haircut for quite some time. This was all right in the winter, but in the summer the darn flies would walk across your head and wake you up if you laid down for a little nap. No matter how often you chased them away, they came right back. It was rather frustrating, trying to get some sleep in the daytime.

I'll never forget the old fishing hole where my brother Frank and I use to fish. I believe it is still there today. At nine o'clock we would bring out the lunch for Dad and Joe and then we would fish to see the old cork bob up and down as the fish nibbled on the bait. Summer meant some work and heat, but it was also lots of fun.

One day, Dad took us fishing and we had a swell time. My Dad was quite a clown when he got started. He used to torment us kids in the summertime, when we went barefoot, by spitting tobacco juice on our toes. Of course we didn't like it, but he laughed so it was okay.

Have you ever watched a little calf nurse at its mother's side, or a litter of little piggies get their dinner while their mother lays on her side so they all can reach? Have you ever come upon a nest of baby bunnies and watch them scamper off through the grass? Did you ever gaze into a bird's nest and count the tiny eggs; blue and brown ones, some speckled, all colors, not much bigger than a jelly bean? Only a country lad with bare feet, freckled face, tattered straw hat, and a merry whistle on his lips sees these things as he strolls through the fields on an errand or a casual walk. What happy days those were when money, war, toys, or trouble were no concern of mine, while I had the whole world for enjoyment.

School reopened the day after the Assumption Holyday, unless it fell on a Thursday. Then, school would open on the following Monday. Vacation was two months long, from June 16 to August 16. The weather was still plenty hot, but people didn't regard the weather like they do now. When the time came to do a certain thing, it was done regardless of the weather, and kids weren't the sissies like today that they can't walk a couple blocks to school, summer or winter. Of course, if it rained too hard, we missed that day. All in all, summer was a wonderful season.

WE GO TO A BARBECUE

In the summer of 1900 when I was eleven years old, my family and I went to a country barbecue. Joe was working as a machine hand on a trashing machine near Poseyville, when he heard that Fr. Schaff of the St. Francis parish was having a barbecue sometime in August, in Wilson's woods. When Joe came home that Saturday evening, he told us about it. Mother asked, "What in the world is a barbecue?" That was something no one in our neighborhood had ever heard of, so Joe explained the whole procedure. The object of the barbecue was to raise money for the St. Francis parish. Dad and Fr. Schaff were good friends so when the day came we all went. Of course, I got my usual quarter to spend.

When the day of the barbecue finally approached, our neighbor's peacock began to cry. It was a common belief in those days that a crying peacock meant bad weather within twenty-four hours. It seldom failed that this darn bird didn't start to raise a rumpus a day or two before we were to go somewhere on a special occasion. I often wished I had that bird by the neck for just one minute. His omen failed more often than it hit, but there was always the possibility that he might be right and this caused the anxiety.

There were ten of us in our family then, and as we had no rig large enough to carry all of us, we went in the wagon. We had only one spring seat so we kids sat on boards laid across the wagon box with a horse blanket laid on top so it wouldn't be so hard. You can imagine how long it took to get all the little ones ready and dressed in their Sunday best and keep them clean until we were ready to leave. We were checked for dirty hands, necks, and ears, and our hair had to be combed just so. Children were the pride of the parents and we had to make a good showing before our neighbors and friends. It was my job to see to it that my sisters kept clean while Mother and Mary dressed. With white petticoats and dresses, that was quite a job, as one of them was sure to ask for a drink of water and would spill some of it on themselves, or get hold of the stove poker or something else dirty. In time, everybody was ready, we all piled into the wagon, and we were off for Wilson's Woods and the barbecue.

It was about two and a half miles from our house and it was a hot day. The yellow dust was inches deep on the road and was as fine as talcum powder. The road was narrow and all along the side, the grass and bushes were covered with this yellow dust. Looking across an open field you could see the heat shimmer like a bowl of Jell-O. Now and then a small whirlwind would start across a plowed field, raising the yellow dust in a spiral like a waterspout at sea. Butterflies were hovering in the air as though suspended by invisible threads, while overhead, a condor was gliding back and forth on a hot air mass without ever using its wings. These signs were considered an omen for continued dry weather. So much for the neighbor's peacock!

It took about forty-five minutes to drive there, and when we arrived it looked like the movie "Cheaper by the Dozen", as everybody for miles around was there and all curious to see what a barbecue was like. Did I eat any barbecue sandwiches? With them selling for ten cents each and me with a quarter spending money to last all afternoon, what do you think? There were many other things to spend it on, and besides, I could get meat and bread at home every day. Peanuts, crackerjack, pop, and a chance on the wheel came only once a year. To a young fellow like me, a quarter doesn't go too far and I had to make it last all afternoon. I was very fortunate, though, as many kids didn't get more than a dime on such occasions. I knew a neighbor boy who went on a picnic with a bare nickel. He bought a box of popcorn and drank water. People those days had little money and with a large family, ten to twenty cents each was a lot. That day, I won a pencil-box with a lead pencil, a slate pencil, a pen holder, and a small ruler in it, and all for a nickel. I was proud of my luck!

Mother and Mary had the care of the girls, and Dad was helping in the booth as Frank and I went our way. About three o'clock, all the dry signs had failed and the peacock had won. The sky began to darken, and thunder could be heard in the distance, but it changed course and all we had was a wee sprinkle. Soon, the sun was out again and the barbecue went on. About an hour before sundown, Mother was ready to go home and started to get us all together. I finally found Frank and we were all set to go. My parents would not stay for the fireworks in the evening, but we were satisfied with the fun we had in the afternoon. By the time we came home it was dusk as we still had all the chores to do. We had seen a barbecue and enjoyed it. This was the only time that our whole family went to anything like this.

When I was about eleven years old, we went to a church social, with booths, soft drinks, etc. In the evening they had the "Passion Play" movie. Yes, I was allowed to stay and see it. It was shown in the church and the admission was ten cents for children, and twenty-five cents for adults.

The movie-machine was a large cumbersome affair, with large gas tanks for the light, as there was no electricity in the country then. I had to go upstairs where we sat during Mass on Sunday. I had a good seat and enjoyed it immensely. It was no comparison to present day movies as it was quite jumpy, but when you have never seen anything like it before, you think it is really great and, considering the time period, it was something worthwhile to see. Poor Mother; as always, she was at home with the younger children and couldn't see it then. About a year or two later, they showed the movie again at a neighboring parish and we children talked Mother and Dad into going, so she finally saw it too.

When I was a little fellow, there were no amusements in the country such as shows, and there were no movies of any kind as yet in theaters, except for the "Passion Play" movie that I mentioned earlier. Once in a while, though, a medicine show would come to St. Wendel and I will try to describe one to you.

I was about nine or ten years old when I saw my first medicine show. It was held in Raben's old warehouse. The admission price was ten cents for children and about twenty-five cents for adults, and there were just ordinary benches to sit on. The show started out with one man giving a rousing talk on their medicines they had to sell (hence medicine show). They had liniments and elixirs that were good for anything that ailed you, from tapeworm to rheumatism, and headaches to ingrown toenails. After a good talk on the ailments of humanity and the healing properties of their remedies, a couple of men would go through the crowd and try to sell as many bottles as possible. Strange to say, they often sold quite a few. After this, the show would start.

It usually started with a magician (they called them slight-of-hand men, then) who performed some pretty good tricks with cards, ropes, and what have you. Then, the minstrels would come on with the black-faced men and the interlocutor. Oh, it was really funny, especially for a group of hicks who had never seen anything like it before. It was well worth the admission price, and some folks even got rid of their rheumatism . . . honest!

Once, my cousin saw one of these shows where a fellow burned some five-dollar bills and restored them to their original state. When I tried to tell her that it was all a fake, she got really angry at me, claiming that she had seen it and that no one could tell her that it didn't happen. Well, what do you think? Did it happen?

One time, Dad was going to take all of us to see a large circus in Evansville. We were going early so we could see the parade. The wagon was all ready to go, but shortly after we got up in the morning it began to thunder in the west. It would have been foolish for my parents to start on a sixteen-mile drive in an open wagon with a family of children, so they waited to see what the weather would do. If it cleared up, we could leave later and still see the circus performance, although we would miss the parade. Well, the weather didn't clear up until it was too late to go, so we missed the circus. Shortly after noon the sun came out and we didn't have any rain for several days. What a disappointment! Just when we were about to see something spectacular, the weather spoiled it for us.

Those days, a kid in the country had few opportunities to see anything but what went on in the neighborhood. To be invited to an old-fashioned apple-pealing, where we pealed about three bushels of apples for the next day's apple-butter cooking, was quite an event and thoroughly enjoyed. As I said earlier, people in the country created their own amusement or they had none.

FOOD AND EATING

To begin with, let us remember there were no self-serve or super-markets in those days. All food was purchased at the corner store or at public markets. In the country, the general store had a grocery department along with the rest of the merchandise.

There also was no refrigeration as we know it today. In the winter, ice was made and many of the stores had their own icehouse where they stored their supply of ice, or they bought it from the brewery wagon when he delivered beer to the saloon. It was customary then to have a saloon and grocery as a combined business. Lake ice was for sale in Detroit as late as the 1920's, when ice machines and the increase in electric refrigerators and the Public Health Authorities stopped it's usage.

In the city, with the exception of baking powder, baking soda, sardines, salmon, and Arbuckle Brothers and McClain's XXXX Coffee, groceries were mostly sold in bulk and were measured or weighed when purchased. I am sure you have heard of the cracker-barrel Politician. Well, I have seen many groceries, but I have yet to see a cracker barrel. Sugar, coffee, and bean barrels, but not crackers. I can remember back seventy years, and at that time crackers were packed in wooden boxes in our part of the country. Spices were in canisters and cookies were also in wooden boxes. The cartons with the glass tops came out much later. The only form of cookies packed in little individual cartons that I can recall were graham crackers and Zu-Zu Ginger Snaps. Cheese came in large pieces and was kept in a screened container to protect it from flies. Oatmeal was the main cereal as Kellogg's had no cereal that I know of, but Kellogg's Corn Flakes came out after the turn of the century where we lived. It was the first ready-to-eat cereal I ever saw.

There were no vegetable counters loaded with fresh produce as we have today. Cabbage, celery, turnips, potatoes, sweet-potatoes, apples, and a few oranges and bananas constituted the variety of produce available in most groceries, unless you went to the market.

Mother usually bought the non-roasted coffee and roasted it herself in a bread pan in the oven. It was two cents a pound cheaper that way. Once a container was opened in the store it remained that way until it was empty, often without a cover or protection against dust and rodents. Once, I saw a cat sleep in a box of bulk tea. You can imagine the picnic mice had in a grocery those days. In the city, the bread was unwrapped, and the milk was delivered in open cans from a wagon drawn by a horse. The milkman had three dippers for one-half pint, one pint, and one-quart pours. The housewife went outside with her pan, dish, or pitcher, and the milkman would measure the amount she wanted with one of his long-handled dippers and pour it into her receptacle. To do this on a windy day would create quite a mess.

Most people had a large shopping basket as the stores didn't supply large bags as they do today. Sauerkraut, pickles, pickled meat, and fish were all in open barrels. Everybody had a one-gallon kerosene can with a pouring spout with which to fill the lamps, since very few houses had gas lights. Kerosene was twelve cents a gallon. All goods were packed in wooden boxes regardless of their nature. During the cold weather, as late as 1914, you would see paper boys on the corner with their cans of fire keeping them warm. This fire was kept going with boxes he picked up in the back of the stores where they were thrown by the store owner. I warmed myself many times with these fires while waiting for the streetcar.

In the city, the housewife didn't shop like she does today. She bought whatever she needed for that day and that as all. Those who had a phone called the store and had it delivered. Most groceries had delivery service those days. All groceries had a large coffee mill with two wheels and the grocer would grind your coffee if you wanted it ground. Mother always ground her own at home, as well as the spices. She also bought nutmegs in the whole and grated it as she used it with a little grater made especially for that purpose. Salt was also sold from a barrel by the pound, as lard and butter were sold from tubs. A & P did this as late as the mid-1930's. After reading the fore-going, you can see that nearly all food was sold from open packages and thus exposed constantly to dust, vermin, and rodents. You can well understand why, in 1906, the United States enacted the Pure Food and Drug Act, which governs and regulates the manufacture and packaging of all foods, drugs, and medicines in the United States.

Now that we have seen how city folk purchased their food, let us take a look at the farmer's larder, which is a room or cupboard where meat and other foods are kept.

When I was a little fellow, it was the belief by many city folks that all farmers had to eat was sauerkraut, sow-belly, and beans.

Well, let's see how true that statement really was at our house. In the winter, we had all kinds of fresh pork. Let's start with spareribs and see how Mother prepared these. Have you ever eaten them with sauerkraut, mashed potatoes, boiled navy or lima beams, bread and butter, or fresh cornbread with country sorghum, preserves, apple-butter, and then top that off with a piece of cream, custard, cottage cheese, evaporated peach or apple pie? Doesn't sound bad, does it? Or maybe Mother decided to bake the spareribs in the oven with rich brown gravy or fry them on top of the stove with rich gravy. That sounds pretty good too. Then there were three kinds of sausage, pickled pork, smoked ham, or fresh pork roast. My Dad would cut fresh pork shoulders in slabs about two inches thick. These my Mother would roast and then pack in earthen crocks and cover them with hot lard. Whenever she wanted to have pork roast, she heated a piece of this meat on top of the stove in a large skillet as we had pork roast as good as you can get anywhere.

For vegetables during the winter months we had cabbage, turnips, and canned tomatoes, while in the summer we had all kinds of fresh vegetables. If the cold didn't kill the fruit, we had apples, blackberries, grapes, peaches, and cherries, all canned for winter, and all fresh right off the tree in the summer.

Just in back of our house was a black raspberry patch. These ripened in July, and it was my job in the morning to pick them. Mother would cook them, put them in a large porcelain dish, and set it on the windowsill to cool. Never once was this dish knocked off. We also had one dish of goose berries. With these, Mother made pies, and were they delicious. In the front yard we had a wild-goose plum tree. It's the only one I have ever seen. The fruit is quite large and strawberry-red. We would gather them every morning and Mother would make pies with some, and jelly or preserves with the rest. She also canned quite a few, but without adding sugar, as they were very tart and needed a lot of sugar to sweeten them. By leaving out the sugar, she would lose only the fruit if a can spoiled. In the winter, she used them in pies.

In those days, when children were seen but not heard, it was the custom that when we had company and there wasn't enough room for all of us to sit around the table, we children had to wait until the adults were through eating. Sometimes, we kids got pretty hungry as we would come to the door and look in. Mother would tell us that they were just about through eating and it wouldn't be long. Of course, someone else would tell another new story and it seemed as though they would never finish. I always felt that if they did more eating and less talking, they could be finished a lot sooner. It seems that the older folks those days didn't regard children like they do today.

We always had a number of spring roosters which we ate ourselves, either roasted, or fried with dumplings. Every fall, as soon as the weather got cool, Dad bought a quarter of beef and we would have home-made beef soup with rice, barley, or ravioli. It has all the modern canned varieties of soup beat in taste. Once in a while, when the men were not working hard, Mother would make a large dish of corn-meal mush and we had an old-fashioned German supper, which was mush and milk. Some of the mush would set until the next morning and Mother would fry it nice and brown and, combined with old country sorghum, made a delicious breakfast. We also had some kind of pie at least twice a week, plus the coffee cake every weekend. Yes, we had nearly everything the city folks had, plus some things that they didn't have.

This reminds me of a story I once heard in my youth. It seems a farmer was cleaning the pig sty when a city salesman came along trying to sell some new gadget to him. The farmer, who was wearing his boots, didn't mind walking in a little mud, while the salesman, trying to protect his highly polished shoes, tip-toed from one dry spot to another while giving his sales talk. The farmer didn't seem to be interested, until the salesman remarked, "I sure wouldn't like to be a farmer with all the dirt and mud you have to put up with." The farmer replied, "Well, we may have the dirt on the outside, but you city folk have it on the inside. You see, when we want chicken for dinner, we kill a young one, while we sell the old rooster and clucking hens to the city where you folks gobble them up. If we want some fruit we pick it off the tree, while you city folk buy the stale stuff in the store." By this time the salesman didn't know what to say and he left the old farmer to his task of cleaning his pig sty while he went looking for a new prospect.

Yes, this is just a story, but there is some truth in it too, more so fifty years ago than now. Any good cook could make a variety of very tasty meals with an assortment of meats, vegetables, and fruits as we had.

OUR NEIGHBORS

About one block below our house was a little wood bridge. It was only a few feet wide so when a horse-pulled rig crossed it, it's hoofs would hit the floor of the bridge about twice before the wheels of the rig would. It sounded like "tap-tap brrrrrr", and the rig was across. We could hear it in the house and it was sort of a signal that a neighbor was passing. Since we knew most of the horses in the neighborhood, we could tell who was going by.

Our nearest neighbor was the Bravy Family. They lived about three blocks from our house. In the winter, when there were no bushes to obstruct the view, we could see into their yard from our kitchen window. They had two boys and two girls at home, and two sons who were married. All of the children were older than me. After Mr. Bravy died, Mrs. Bravy moved away, and a family by the name of Craft moved into their place. They had two boys and three girls. One girl was older than me, while the other children were all younger. The oldest boy was about three months younger than I and we became very good friends. He was at our house quite often, as Mr. Craft worked for my Dad at times and the boy came along. Mother and us kids learned most of our English through this family. They were the only English-speaking family in the neighborhood. With the exception of the Craft boy, these were my only playmates in the whole neighborhood. All the other children were either too young or too old for me to play with.

The next neighbor was Fred Schweikhart, Jr. They had one boy and one girl, both quite a bit younger than I. A quarter of a mile farther up the road lived the old Fred. They also had a boy and girl, still living at home, and both much older than me.

These were the people that had that darn peacock with the nose for weather. They also had chickens, ducks, geese, turkeys, guinea's, pigeons, and martins. They had the prettiest martin house I have ever seen, and lots of martins used it. I often stopped when I passed there and watched the fowl, especially when that peacock was fanning his tail, or some turkey gobbler was strutting his stuff with his tail all fanned out and gobbling like mad. It was also interesting to watch the martins come and go and chase the sparrows from the house. They also had a little black devil of a dog. I believe he would have torn me to pieces if he had ever gotten out on the road. We had to pass their house on our way to part of our farm. Every time I passed, that dog would be there snarling and barking like mad.

The next house on the road was Grandpa Schmitt, my Mother's Father. It was a mile from our place. My Uncle Adam moved there after Grandpa's death. Uncle Adam was my favorite uncle. About twice a year I was allowed to go there on a Sunday afternoon, but I had to be home on time to do my chores. I was allowed to stay for supper, but right after it was over, I had to be on my way home.

Just a half mile across the field lived the Seib family, which included the old folks and their married son. By the time the son and his wife celebrated their tenth wedding anniversary they had nine boys, all of them too young for me to play with. Mr. Seib, Sr., was a real German immigrant. He always made his own wine, raised his own tobacco, and always smoked a curved stem pipe with a lid to prevent sparks from flying. He never used profane language, but instead would say "sabramant". In German this sounded real funny to us and we often had a good laugh over it. The Seib family had only forty acres of land, but in 1901, Dad sold twenty acres to them. A picket fence separated the two tracts of land. Dad had bought forty-one acres just across the road from our farm, which included the house in which the Craft family lived. The twenty acres he sold to the Seib's had two creeks running through it and a big hill that couldn't be cultivated, so he was glad to sell it.

A quarter of a mile east of us lived John Spahn and his wife. They had two children, both much younger than I. A little farther up the road lived Mrs. Greulich. She was a widow and had two boys and four girls at home. One boy was totally blind, and all were much older than me. They also had two black devils of dogs. I was sent there once to get something, and I thought they would tear the fence down to get at me. One of the girls came out and made them behave. Then there was Frank Schaefer who lived about a mile through the field from us. He was a widower and had two boys and a girl at home, all much older than me.

North of us lay what was called the Big Creek Flats. The nearest house there was over a mile from us on the other side of the creek. It was here where the English-speaking settlement began and for miles beyond everybody spoke English. All the German speaking people lived south of us. After I reached my teens, I often worked for some of these English-speaking neighbors for a day or two at a time, and in this way, I earned some spending money. Some of these people were Catholic, while others were Lutheran, and we never had any neighbor trouble with any of them. My folks visited back and forth with most of them and they also helped each other in thrashing. The senior Mrs. Seib baptized my younger brother when he was a day old, as he was quite ill and could not be taken to St. Wendel's for Fr. Pfeiffer to baptize him.

People in those days stayed pretty much to themselves. When you met one of the neighbors, you might exchange a few words about the latest news, the weather, or some comment about the crops, but that was all. In case of any serious illness or emergency, your nearest neighbors were the first to be consulted. They, in turn, would render whatever assistance he was able to give, be it day or night. Without a telephone to contact him, things had to be really serious before a neighbor was ever bothered. If help was needed, one of the older children was sent to ask the wife to come and give whatever assistance she was able to offer. That's when Grandma's remedies were applied, and many a doctor bill was avoided by so doing. With the nearest doctor three miles away and no way to contact him, all the known skills were used before the husband went for the doctor. I know our present-day doctors do not approve of this way of treating sick people, but those days it was the accepted practice and everybody did it. Yes, many things have changed since I was a small boy, some for the better, and others for worse. I am certain that in sixty-five years from now many of our present practices will be just as outmoded as those of the Nineteen-Hundreds are today. Time changes many things, even people.

MOMENTS OF FEAR

On order for you to realize what the following events meant to me, let me say that in those days, when I was a little lad, children of my age were not aware of things as they are today. Consequently, it didn't take much to create a fear in a child's mind.

The fear of fire was especially dwelt upon at all times. The matches of those days were very dangerous, and many fires were started through the careless use of them. The head of the match, when struck, exploded at times and pieces of fire would fly several feet. Lace curtains and similar flimsy material could easily be set afire by them. Rats or mice could also fire the matched by chewing on the heads. We kept our matches in a cast-iron safe with a lid as a precaution. This, naturally, instilled a deep fear into our young minds. One night, when I was about nine years old, old Fred Motz's house burned down. It was a log house, so it burned for a long time. It was about one mile from our place and, though there was no danger, we kids were quite scared.

One time, Joe set fire to an old stump in the meadow. The fire got out of control and burned over much of the meadow. Dad wasn't home, so Mother rang the dinner bell which summoned him home from the woods where he was working. He took a team of horses and plowed furrows around the fire, which stopped it. It burned part of the rail fence and I was scared it would get up to the barn.

One Sunday, late in the fall, the family went somewhere, leaving Joe and me alone at home. We had walked to Mass, and on the way home, we saw clouds of smoke rise from what looked to be coming from the woods. We started running and, coming closer to home, saw that our woods were on fire and was heading toward the pigs. We changed clothes in a hurry, grabbed pitchforks, and went to put out the fire. The fence was already burning in one place. We put this out and then proceeded to kill the rest of the fire. I don't remember how long it took us, but we did get it all out and our pigs were safe.

Because of the lightening and heavy thunder, thunderstorms meant terror to me. We saw three barns burn in one night that had been struck by lightning during one storm. Once, lightning struck a wheat stock close to our house. It immediately burst into flames. We had several large trees on our farm and most of them had been struck by lightning at least once. Mother taught me a little prayer to say during a storm. I said it many times in my young life. It went as follows, "From lightening, hail, and destructive storms, protect us, O Lord."

One Easter Sunday, during the sermon, lightning struck the church steeple. It was a real bad storm and I am sure I wasn't the only one in church that was scared. Fortunately, there was no fire. On another occasion, one Sunday afternoon, we kids were home alone when we had a severe storm with torrential rain, hail, and strong winds. All the creeks were flooded, and Dad and Mother had to stay all night at the neighbors, as the water was too high to go through. We were all scared that time.

One afternoon, we watched a tornado as it passed our place about a half mile distance. We could see the debris fly through the air. About a half hour later, Uncle Adam came by and told us that at the Frank Geode's farm, the old Grandpa, who was in his eighties, a man in his twenties, and a four year old boy had been killed by the tornado. Had it not been for the kitchen stove and a strong table, the whole family would have been killed. These two items prevented the one wall from completely collapsing and the rest of the family was able to crawl out unhurt. The day after the tornado, Frank, Mary, a neighbor girl and I drove over to see the place where the people were killed. All the buildings except for the granary were completely destroyed. Several horses and cows were also killed, and machinery was smashed. One of their schoolbooks was found in a corn field ten miles away.

One evening, in the summer of 1896, Joe was sitting on the back porch to remove his shoes, which was customary with him after following a plow all day. About this time, Mother and Mary came up from the barn-lot with the evenings milking. Joe got up from the porch, grabbed an old-fashioned candle stick with its homemade tallow candle, and proceeded towards the cellar to place the candle on the steps to help in taking the milk down in the cellar. Just as he was about to raise the cellar door, he leaped back and let out a terrifying scream. Dangling on his left foot was a copperhead snake, a species of the rattler, and the most venomous snake in the area. Mary quickly handed him a hoe from the fence nearby, which he killed the snake with. While Mother wrapped tourniquet's on his foot and leg to cut off the circulation, Mary ran to the neighbor and summoned Mrs. Bravy, while Frank and I ran up the road to meet

Dad, who we knew would be coming home from thrashing at a neighbors. It was just about dusk when we met Dad and Mr. Bravy a little ways up the road. In the meantime, Mrs. Bravy and Mother had applied all the home remedies they knew of while Joe was suffering extreme pain. His foot and leg had swollen to twice its size by then. Dad quickly hitched a horse to a rig and took Joe to the nearest doctor, three miles away.

Some of the home remedies were soaking the foot in a dish of sweet milk. They also opened a live chicken and he stuck his foot into the opening. The warmth of the chicken was supposed to draw the poison out of the wound. I am sure there were other remedies. Sounds silly? Well, that was 1896, long before the days of sulfa, cortisone, and all the new drugs we have today. Joe had some internal medicine and also had some with which he bathed his foot and leg several times a day. He was confined to bed about three weeks. The snake was only about two feet long. Had it been full size in which the venom would have been greater, he might not have lived through it. The following summer, the poison stored in his system reacted again and he was laid up again for about two weeks. To think that we children had been playing around the cellar all evening made us shudder. A couple of us could have been bitten by that snake!

After Joe's snake bite, there were days when he didn't feel so good, especially his leg. He saw the doctor, but it seemed no one knew what ailed him. One doctor recommended bicycle riding, so he bought a used one and learned to ride it. Later, Frank also learned to ride it. One evening, Frank took it out on the road and somehow must have fallen, because he ended up dislocating his knee. He was not able to walk for several weeks and, as this was the busy time of the year, it was not good. This ended the bike riding and Joe traded it to a neighbor boy for a watch and three dollars.

Due to a family misunderstanding, one of our neighbors committed suicide with poison. He had taken ill, and his family ended up leaving him in a huff. My Dad and the neighbors took care of him during his illness, not knowing about the presence of the poison in the house. Of course, Dad and Mother discussed what went on there, and since we children were always around we heard most of it. This was quite eerie for a small kid. Another man was found dead in bed with a gun at his side. The coroner called it suicide, but a number of circumstances pointed towards murder. There were no investigations, so it remained a suicide.

Once, when my sister Cecilia was quite small, she got a buttonhook stuck in her teeth. Naturally, she was scared when she couldn't dislodge it and started to cry. All of us kids cried with her. Mother tried to take it out but couldn't, so she called Dad after a little while. He managed to loosen it and took it out.

For a while, one of our neighbors had spooks at their house. First, two large dogs could be heard outside at night. Then, they could hear weird noises, like someone walking across the long porch in front of the house, along with slamming doors, etc. It got so bad that they asked the neighbors for protection. Dad went several times with his shotgun, but no one came while the men were there. One night, the dogs did come, but no one else. The haunting continued, so one night many men went over to catch the culprit, even men from St. Wendel, with rifles, shotguns, and revolvers. That night, two strange men came into Coudret's Saloon inquiring about the spooks. Mr. Coudret, not thinking, let the cat out of the bag by telling them that if the spook showed up that night he would get a hot reception, as the whole neighborhood was there waiting for the spooks to show up. That ended the spook scare. They were not heard of anymore.

As I said in the beginning, children then were not as mature as children today. Anything out of the ordinary was a terrible thing to us and caused fear in our little hearts and minds.

AUTUMN

This is a beautiful season of the year, especially in the country when the leaves begin to turn color. Big Creek Flats was mostly woods at that time, so whichever way we looked we could see gorgeous colors. The mornings were cool now and barefoot time was over., while a vest or light coat was in order. Mother brought out her little shawl which she wore over her shoulders until after breakfast. She called it her breakfast shawl. The days were much shorter now and instead of eating an early supper, the men stayed in the field until sundown. Because of this, we ate supper by lamplight.

Wheat sowing had come and often, after supper, Dad and Joe would blue-stone the wheat seed for the next day's sowing, while I held a lantern so they could see. Bluestone was obtained by mixing a quantity of blue vitriol with water. With the aid of a sprinkling can, this was sprinkled over the wheat, then raked through it with a garden rake until the whole area was thoroughly covered. This was supposed to prevent some type of disease in the wheat the following summer.

The grapes, late peaches, and all of the apples were ripe now. These apples were the Winesaps, Ben-Davis, and Roman Beauties, plus a few on the old swing-tree where we hung our rope swings. The latter type were so juicy that it ran down your chin when you took a bite. We had a late peach tree in the garden. They were quite small and had clingstones. Every evening I would pick some and put them in my school bag for the next day. They were so sweet and juicy. Because of their small size Mother never used them and Dad finally cut the tree down. I sure missed them the next fall.

Persimmons were also ripe at that time and we would get a pail full to eat. They have a taste all their own. Opossums and raccoons are very fond of them and will go a long way to get them. Sometimes we made cider with them by mashing them, place the mash in an open top barrel and adding three parts water to one-part mash. When the mash rises to the top, the cider is ready to drink. It has the color of champagne with a pleasant taste and is non-alcoholic.

Autumn is also sweet cider and apple-butter time. To cook a kettle of apple-butter is a two-day job. All the apples had to be peeled and cut up the day before, and usually the cider was boiled some to remove the excess water. The next morning, the apples were added and these had to be stirred constantly to keep them from sticking to the bottom and scorching. A copper kettle was used and, as it was very thin, very little fire was needed. It was an all-day job.

Mother and Mary did the milking while the men did the evening chores. I was the baby-sitter, and usually hungry as a bear. Sometimes it seemed they would never finish the milking, especially when I couldn't stop the baby from crying.

Autumn was also time to cut corn for shock-fodder. We kids would cut the corn and place it in piles, and Dad and Joe would set it up in shocks. Once, I cut my foot and I wasn't able to wear a shoe for a few weeks.

Breakfast was eaten by lamplight. If Mother forgot to put out the lamp and, later, would come in the summer-kitchen to find it still burning, she would say, "Well, I am burning a hole in the day again!" Mornings were getting pretty chilly and about the last week in October we would move the cook stove and things back to the winter-kitchen again. I had to clean all the soot out of and under the stove in order to give it a good draught. This would allow it to bake well during the winter. The two downstairs bedrooms were papered, but the walls in the kitchen were just white-washed, so it received a good dusting, and that was all.

Often on Sunday afternoons, I slung a grain sack over my shoulder and headed for the woods in search of hickory nuts. By now the trees were all in their best dress suit. Orange, lemon, red, different shades of brown, and various greens. How I enjoyed a walk through the woods with the leaves under my feet. If I was lucky, I would get quite a few hickory nuts, but if someone else beat me to them I came home with an empty bag. I didn't have overalls then and my cotton pants would gather all kinds of burs. One, called Spanish Needle, would go right through the cloth, break off, and scratch you for days. Once in a while I would scare up a covey of quail or a rabbit, or see a squirrel scamper up a tree.

The sun was setting low in the sky now, and the summer birds were nearly gone. There would only be a few still lingering on a bush in the fence row, singing one last song before they too departed for a warmer climate. Large flocks of wild geese and ducks could be seen winging their way south and, the not too distant frost was in the air. You could hear the quail call their mates in the woods and weed fields and see the red-headed woodpecker flit from tree to tree, looking for a few grubs in the rotten tops of an oak or gum tree. In the morning, hundreds of crows would fly over our house on their way to the melon fields for food. In the evening, they would return to their roosting ground in the German Township woods, about eighty miles distant. Sometimes there were just a few in a group, and then hundreds of them in one flock. There were literally thousands of these birds going back and forth every day.

Waking across a field, the floating cobwebs would sail past or encircle your face and neck. Have you ever seen one of those large golden spiders in her nest, suspended in a corner of a rail fence, with the cold dew on it? Soon, the frost would drive Mrs. Spider into her winter home.

The last job in the garden was the digging and hilling-in of the turnips, and planting the potato onions. After hilling-in the turnips, the hill was covered with straw so the ground wouldn't freeze so hard. This would allow us to dig some out when we wanted them. By now, all plant life had been killed by the frost and the garden looked pretty bare. Potato onions have no seeds and can be raised only by planting onion-sets, like planting tulip bulbs. Mother raised a radish with the turnips. These she pealed in the evening and sliced them quite thin. After this, she placed a little salt between the slices. This would draw out some of the juice so that they would not be so strong. We enjoyed eating them for breakfast with eggs, meat, and fried potatoes. I can still taste them. I have never seen them in stores up here.

Corn husking was the last big job of the season. Some of the shock-fodder we shucked in the field, while some of it we did in the barn. Dad would haul in a few loads of fodder and then, on Saturday or rainy days, we could shuck this in the barn. At planting time, Dad would mix a few red grains with the rest, so it was always a thrill for us kids when we found a red ear. The competition between us kids was very keen, not that we received a prize, but just to see who would find the first one.

The sorghum was also cut then, to be used for the mill and cooker to have it ground and cooked into molasses. This was quite a process to watch. The cane was passed through a set of steel rollers and the juice pressed out. From the mill, it passed through a hose to a series of tin pans mounted on a four wheeled truck which was fitted with a fire box and extending the full length of the pans. This was fired with old fence rails and the juice was transferred from pan to pan until it became the finished molasses. One year we had one hundred and twenty-five gallons, most of which we sold for twenty-five cents a gallon.

With the corn all in we were now ready for winter. Often, late in the day, a strong wind began to blow. The cows and pigs would run and jump like a bunch of kids at play. You could hear the wind roar through the woods. Dad would come into the house and remark, "The way the wind sounds, we will get some cold weather!" Quite often he was right, and by morning everything was frozen solid. Out would come the gloves and the cap with the pull-down ear flaps, but no overcoat, rubbers, overshoes, or sweater. These things were not made in children's sizes then. Pants were a little below the knees with long black stockings, and ankle high shoes with buttons instead of lace. If the button hook was displaced, you hunted for it as you couldn't button your shoes without one. No Mackinaws either. A suit vest and coat was about all you had. Our road was hilly, so if we got too cold we ran down the hill. That brought the blood in circulation and warmed us up. I don't know how we got through the winter walking three miles, twice a day, and often in zero weather. Coming home we walked due west, right into the wind and cold. Everybody had horses or mules, but no one ever took their children to school. It just wasn't done. The custom was for the children to walk to school and they did just that in all kinds of weather. Sometimes the roads were almost impassable, and you could walk faster than drive, so often on Sundays we walked to Mass too.

About the first week of December the weather got quite cold at night, and it was time to butcher the pigs for meat for the coming year. It didn't take long for us kids to get home from school the day we butchered, as we wanted to see as much as possible.

My three Uncles - Ike, Joe, and Adam - always helped with the butchering. Together, they and my Dad owned the grinders and stuffers necessary for the job. Each had a large iron kettle. These kettles, along with the large table on which most of the work was done, plus some extra tubs, were all brought in a day or two before we butchered. The kettles were hung on a strong pole, and all were filled to the top with water. A large load of old fence rails were hauled up for fire wood. Straw and kindling wood was put around the kettles and were ready to light the next morning. Extra barrels of water were placed nearby for quick uses. The spices were all ground, an extra dish of salt was brought up, and everything was ready for the next day.

We were up about dawn, and Dad lit the fires early, as it takes a long time to heat water in an open kettle on a cold morning. About dawn, my uncles would arrive. By daylight, the water was hot and the butchering started. This was done in two trips. About three pigs were killed during the first trip. When these had been cleaned and hung up, the remainder were killed. Uncle Joe was the shooter, and Uncle Adam was the sticker. Uncle Joe used an old muzzle-loading rifle. I can still see that old rifle standing in the corner of Mother's bedroom, with the pouch hanging over the muzzle. Although the gun was never loaded, we were always cautioned not to go near it, and we didn't.

After the first pigs were hung up, Uncle Joe would start removing the entrails. This was always his job. It seems each man had his particular work and knew just when and how to do it. The entrails were brought into the house where the fat was removed, and they were separated. This was a messy job and was done on the table by the women. After the second group of pigs were hung up, all the heads were removed, cut up, and placed on the large table to cool. This meat was the primary ingredient for the liver sausage and headcheese. While the meat was boiling, the men cleaned the casings. Usually, my older brother was the fireman. It was his duty to keep the fire going, to keep the meat boiling, and skim off the scum that gathered on top with a large skimming ladle. About noon, the casings were all clean and some of the pigs were cut up into the proper pieces. While the meat was cooling, the men were ready for lunch. The lunch menu was the same each year. It consisted of a piece of jowl (a pig's double chin) boiled with sauerkraut, fried pigs brains, navy beans, mashed potatoes, and the usual trimmings that went with it.

After lunch, Uncle Joe started scraping and cutting into proper lengths the large casings. These were washed and scraped several times and cut into eighteen-inch lengths, with one end tied with a string that was long enough to tie the other end, after the sausage had been stuffed. When all these sausages had been stuffed, they were placed in the water used to cook the meat, and slowly simmered for quite some time. This was done to cure the onions and it would also remove some of the excess grease. When they were done, they were laid on the large table to cool. After this, they were hung in the smoke house. Also, after lunch, the rest of the pigs were cut up and two men would start grinding the raw meat for the country sausage, after first grinding the boiled meat for the liver sausage. One good sized onion was used for each pig in the liver sausage, and about one whole liver in all the meat. Too much liver makes the sausage dry. Two different grinders were used as the raw meat was ground much finer than the cooked meat.

By this time, Mother and my Aunt Mary were busy scraping the small casings for the country sausage. This was done with the back of a kitchen knife on a board. When they were finished, the casings were as thin as a plastic bag.

While some of the men were working on the sausages, the rest of the men, and the children who were old enough, were cubing the lard to be rendered the next day. The meat for the headcheese included part of the head, the heart, and the rinds. This was all cut by hand into narrow strips, and some raw meat was also used. This was all stuffed into the stomachs by hand and these, like the liver sausage, were also simmered for a long time. Afterwards, they were laid out to cool, and then pressed by laying a board across them that was weighed down with stones, while they were still warm. They were then hung in the smoke house to be smoked with green hickory wood. This gave them a very good taste. If all went well, we were usually finished by dark.

About nine in the morning, Mother would fix a large pitcher of what she called whisky punch. It was a mixture of good whisky, sugar, nutmeg, and hot water. I had some once, and in about fifteen minutes I was not only warm, I was also dizzy! If we didn't have any cider, Dad would get a keg of beer, and we kids were allowed to have a sample too.

Supper menu never changed and consisted of both kinds of sausage, fried potatoes, cottage cheese and the trimmings, cookies, pie, and donuts. The men usually went home shortly after supper.

Finally, the butchering was done and we had plenty of meat for another year. The next morning, Dad, Mother, and the older children that were not in school started to render the lard and clean up the implements used the day before. Dad also salted down the hams, shoulders, and bacon. After the meat was in salt about six weeks, it was hung in the smokehouse and also smoked with hickory wood until it was brown. Then, it was put into bags and hung up until it was wanted. The bags protected it against flies and vermin. The salt-pork, or pickled-pork as we called it, was the thin part of bacon. This was cut into small pieces and packed into a big earthen crock while a salt brine was poured over it. This brine was made by dissolving salt in water until it was strong enough to float an egg. Then, it was heated to remove the impurities and left to cool. When it was barely lukewarm, it was poured over the meat until it was fully covered.

A few days after butchering, Mother fried down the sausage and shoulders she wanted to keep for the following summer. This gave us sausage and fresh roast pork all summer long. The sausage was usually for Sunday breakfast and the pork for Sunday dinner, as it was quickly heated after we came home from Sunday Mass. Now you know why a farmer's ham and sausage always tastes so good.

It was now about the second week in December and with the butchering done, the farmer was ready to settle down for the winter, which wasn't far off. Thoughts of Christmas were now beginning to come to mind and soon the snow would fly. Although the summer birds were gone and nature was once more falling asleep, I had enjoyed a wonderful summer and fall season. How wonderful nature is when you can see it in its fullness and know how to appreciate and enjoy it. City boys may have a lot to see, but it doesn't compare with nature as I saw it, when I was a little boy in short pants and a dirty face.

WINTER

Winter weather usually started the first week of December, even though it doesn't officially start until the twenty-first. What a thrill it was to look up from our studies in school and discover that it was snowing. I always enjoyed walked home from school in a howling snowstorm. I still enjoy it today. It invigorates my whole body and sort of makes a kid out of me all over again. Sounds silly? Maybe it does, but is it really so silly?

Since we were on central time the days were one hour shorter than they are here in Detroit. The sun rose at eight in the morning and set at four in the afternoon, instead of seven and five like it does here. On cloudy days it was dark by four-thirty in the afternoon. When we left in the morning for school, the stars were still shining brightly, and I admired the beautiful full moon many mornings on our way to school. In the open country, you can see the horizon all the way down in front of you so you can see every star and the moon until it slips below the horizon. Here in the city, you only see the stars that are above the trees and houses. Some of the larger starts are in the lower horizon, so you never see them here in the city. It was fascinating to watch the morning star grow dimmer and dimmer as daylight approached. Then suddenly, the sun popped above the horizon like a big ball of fire, and another day was born. The start of winter meant that Christmas wasn't too far off, and that also brightened out spirits.

We burned wood in both stoves, which meant that the wood-box had to be filled to the top every evening so it would last all the next day. There was also a pile of large chunks for the heating stove in the bedroom. How those stoves would eat up the wood on a cold day.

The heating stove had a small ash pan in front with a sliding lid which served as a draught regulator and cover for the ash pan. Opening this draught gave the stove a full force and the fire burned more vigorously, causing a roar like a locomotive. We used to play train that way, and by opening and closing the lid, we controlled the roar. This represented the train's speed. Sometimes I would get real coal from the pile in the yard that was left over from thrashing. With this, I would start a small fire in the opening between the lid and the door. Then, I would pretend I was the fireman on the train.

If the weather wasn't too bad, the men would work in the woods making fence posts and pickets, plus a good supply of wood for the next year. The wood blocks were hauled home where they were split and piled in rows so they would dry out. Much of the piling was done by us kids. On Saturday, I was allowed to go along to the woods and Dad would let me cut down a little tree about four inches thick. By the time I had it cut down, it looked as though a rat had chewed it off. If I could find some wild grape vines, I would get a dry piece and smoke it as we generally had a fire. Dad would stand by laughing as I blew large clouds of smoke in the air while my tongue burnt as if I had eaten red pepper. Dad was very tolerant at times and would go along with a gag like that.

In the winter, the washing was done in the kitchen. We had a hand-powered machine and with all the boiling and rinsing, it made quite a mess. The clothes were always hung outside, regardless of the season. On cold, windy days, the long underwear would freeze stiff, making it appear as though a lot of ghosts were hanging on the line. The next day was ironing day. Mary would get out the old wooden clothes horse on which she hung the ironed clothes so they would dry out completely before she put them away. Mother always used bluing, which she made herself by dissolving blue vitriol in water and putting it into bottles. One mixing usually lasted a whole year and all the clothes went through the bluing water.

When the weather was bad, the men folk sat around the house, mostly in the kitchen, where we always ate three full meals a day. There was something cooking on the stove most of the time, so we had ample chances to watch food being prepared. No wonder we learned to cook! Sometimes, Dad would sit by the heating stove and read so we kids had to be on our guard and not get too noisy. If we did get too loud, he would open the door, take one look at us over the top of his glasses, and that was the signal to quiet down or else. No words were necessary.

When Mary got tired of having us around, she would get the broom, open all the windows, and start sweeping. She was soon all alone, as we didn't stick around long with all the windows open. She would laugh and call us softies. Just the same, we had a lot of fun. What fun, and sometimes grief, an only child misses while growing up. Sure, I got a licking once in a while because of my brothers and sisters, but never without a warning. The fun we had together far overshadows all the lickings I ever received. Just sitting here and writing this is like living my kid days all over again. I can see the old kitchen just as it was then, with Mother and Mary going about, busy as always.

Although we had a three-mile walk, winter weather seldom kept us home from school, unless it was pouring rain. In a light rain we took an umbrella and went just the same. Yes, we had horses and mules in the stable, but nobody took their children to school. Sometimes, the roads were almost impassable with deep mud, and walking was easier than trying to drive. It just wasn't custom to take the children to school, so we all walked. We didn't have a sleigh, so sleigh rides were out of the question. Joe had made a small sled on which we sometimes went sled riding on a hill in the fields. I never owned any ice skates so I never went skating and, to this day, I don't know how to skate, ice or roller. We had a lot of fun, though, plowing through snow drifts on our way home from school, getting quite wet at times, for which we got a scolding.

Sunday afternoon was a dull time at our house. So, while Dad would be reading the German Catholic paper, and Mother would be reading the Gospels and Epistles of the day, with their explanations, we kids made popcorn balls. While I popped the corn, Mary prepared the molasses and then formed the balls. Once in a great while, she also made a batch of molasses candy. This has to be pulled like taffy while it is still quite hot until it gets stiff. During the pulling, the molasses will turn from a deep brown to a light yellow. On Sunday afternoons, we kids were pretty much on our own, so long as we played without too much noise.

Winter was also sewing time. While Mother was making new garments, Mary was stitching quilt blocks, darning stockings, or doing the weekly patching. Mother made all of our clothes; shirts, underwear, petticoats, and house dresses, which were called "wrappers" then. This was a one-piece garment with buttons in front from the belt up. Petticoats were made of white linen in the summer, and flannel or wool in the winter. I wore home-made drawers until I left home. Sometimes, Mother would rip apart an old dress of hers and make a new one out of it for one of the girls. She would also make a pair of pants for me from on old pair of Dad's. The only clothes that were bought were men's or boy's suits and pants. If you had an older brother or sister, you often wore hand-me-downs, as we called them. I am sure this is still done.

I had a small head when I was younger, compared to other boys my age. A regular boys straw hat was too large for me, so Mother bought me a Buster Brown style hat. Today you may see a little girl wear one on occasion. You can imagine how I felt wearing one of these with a rubber band under my chin to keep it from blowing off on the way to church. I was about ten years old then, but that made no difference. I always tucked the rubber inside the crown as soon as we reached the church, so I wouldn't look too much like a sissy. The way I looked, all I needed was the name of "Percy" to complete the picture. It was the only hat that would fit me, so I wore it and kept quiet. I wore waists with large sailor collars, and I liked them very much. What was a waist and how does it differ from a shirt? A waist was only belt length, with buttons around the belt to which the pants were buttoned, to keep them from falling down. All boys wore them until they started wearing long pants and suspenders. Then, they began to wear shirts. I wore silk ties about four inches wide, which my sister, Mary, always tied for me, and how she could fix up those bows. She was a wonderful sister.

Mother bought unbleached muslin with which she made our sheets. Mother would by the unbleached type as this was cheaper and saved a few cents per sheet. She would wash these and then hang them out on the line and let them bleach in the sun. Many of our pillowcases were flour sacks. After a few washings and boilings, the printing on the sack would disappear, and they were ideal to use because they were nice and soft. All the trimmings from her sewing were saved and these provided the material for the quilt blocks. When Mother or Mary received some expensive cloth from Grandma, she took it to the Waszmer girls and had the dress made. They were professional dressmakers and would do a nice job for about two dollars per dress. Any farmer's wife who did her own sewing and kept up the housework had plenty to do all winter long.

If we came home with a cold or hoarseness, Mother got the goose-grease and quinine mixture and we got a good rubbing on the chest and throat, along with a dose of Dr. Mendenhall's Cold and Chill Cure. If we were no better by morning, we stayed home from school. If we had a cough along with it, we took an elderberry jelly, honey, and butter mix. We also might take rock candy or onion soup and, in a day or two, we were able to go back to school. Nobody called a doctor for a little thing like this. At night we took one of the stockings we had worn all day, turned it inside-out, put it around our throat, and pinned it with a safety pin. It did relieve our coughing. Were these old-fashioned remedies? Yes, and they generally did the trick. They didn't cost $5 for a prescription like today that sometimes don't give much relief.

On real cold days, Dad would come in the house, with his mustache frozen, stomp his feet, and say, "It's damn cold today! Poor cattle. I feel sorry for them outside on a day like this." We had no cow-stable to put them in so they were around the straw stack under a shed. This gave them some protection, but not enough when it was windy and real cold. After we had the new barn, we had a place where they could go when the weather was bad.

When I was still real small, I remember Dad wearing leather boots in winter. These went up to his knees, and when they got wet they would get hard. It required a bootjack to get them off, and a lot of pulling and stomping to get them back on the next morning. A bootjack is a board about six inches wide with a V-cut in one end. A piece of wood about two inches thick is nailed on one side, just in back of the V-cut, to raise it up at that end so you can hook your heal into it. With your other foot, you stand on the other end of the board to hold it down. and then you start to pull until the boot comes off. Every week, Dad greased his boots to keep them soft, more pliable, and waterproof. It helped, but didn't solve the problem altogether. A bootjack was a tool that could be found in every farm those days. In fact, it was a necessity.

Now was the time when all the canned goods, dried fruits, sauerkraut, turnips, and the pickled meat came in handy in the preparation of our daily meals. Sometimes we ate the dried fruit stewed and at other times, Mother made pies with it. She would whip them up good, add spices, and bake them into a lattice top pie. Yum, yum, good! The taste is altogether different from the evaporated fruit you buy in stores. They were much better, by far. Sometimes, Mother added a few raisins which improved the flavor even more. There is no substitute for sun and open air when it comes to drying fruit.

We had no pump in the house, so the water was brought into the house in a cedar pail with three brass hoops. These were kept shining like mirrors at all times. Often after supper, this pail was empty, so if one of us kids wanted a drink of water, one of the older ones had to get a pail of water from the well. Sometimes they were all reading and nobody wanted to go. Sometimes they ended up by pulling straws and the one with the shortest straw had to get the water. Sounds like a lazy trick, doesn't it? Sure it does, but such as the case at times.

Winter was also buck-wheat pancake time. Eaten with country sorghum, they make a real breakfast, one that will stick to your ribs, as we use to say. They are made with about two-parts buckwheat and one-part white flour, set with yeast, and let stand over night to rise. Sometimes it would go over the top if the house was quite warm.

We had the old-fashioned windows with six panes of glass in each window. We had no storm-windows, so often, in cold weather, the water in the kitchen had a sheet of ice on it. Mother would open the oven doors to get all the heat possible, while we kids were huddled close by, trying to get warm. Some cold days, the windows didn't thaw out completely all day.

In the winter, the English people north of us would go fox hunting through our land. We could see the fox with the hounds in close pursuit.

The large woods, which was all virgin timber, was just a quarter mile from our house. At night, we could hear the big horn owls hooting. If a farmer planted any young fruit trees in the fall, he had to wrap them with newspaper at least eighteen inches high to protect them from the rabbits. When the snow is deep and their regular food is covered, they will eat the bark off the young trees. This will kill the trees in spring. One time, Dad found a bevy of quail under a snowbank. They were freezing and starving to death, so he put them in a grain bag, brought them into the house, and put them in the little hall. Here, he fed them until the weather got warmer and they had a chance to recuperate. Then he opened the door and let them all go back to their mode of life. Yes, winters were pretty rugged in those days, but so were the people. They had to be able to live through them and survive.

Dad was seventy-eight, Mother was eighty-five, and my brother Joe was seventy-seven when they passed on to their reward. In 1907, my sister, Mary, joined an Order of Franciscan Nuns at

Oldenburg, Indiana, where she passed on in 1923. My brother, Frank, was seventy-nine last December. I am going on seventy-five and have three younger sisters and a brother still living, all past the sixty-four-year mark.

I hope this book gave you some idea of country life, its hardships, and also its joys. Things on a farm were a lot different during the horse and buggy days than they are now. People had a lot less and made the best of it. People were poor, needed little, and got along with what they had, and most of them were satisfied with what they had. Luxuries did not influence them, nor did they crave for them like people do today. All in all, it wasn't too bad. I know, I was there.

THE END

THE MÜLLER (MILLER) FAMILY TREE

Nicklous Müller, born October 10, 1788, in Darmstadt, Germany.
Katherena Baetz, born March 19, 1793, in Darmstadt, Germany.
Their children:

- Katharina Müller, born July 15, 1820, in Fulda, Hesse, Germany
- John M. Müller, born June 27, 1827 in Darmstadt., Germany.

The Müller's (later Americanized to 'Miller') immigrate to America in the spring of 1832. The ship carrying the Müller family was scheduled to land in New York. However, severe storms blew them so far off course that they were at sea for three months instead of the normal month and a half. Given the long journey, their daily rations for the last two days consisted of a half onion and a cup of water. They eventually landed somewhere in or near the State of Virginia, possibly sailing into the Chesapeake Bay.

Following their arrival, the Müller family they made their way to Wheeling, West Virginia, some 300 miles northwest of their landing point. They stayed in Wheeling until 1834, subsequently traveling west to the Evansville, Indiana, where a large German community had already been established.

After settling in the greater Saint Wendel area, daughter Katharina Müller married notable local resident Wendelen Waszmer. Wendelen and his brother, Marcus, were also from Germany and were instrumental in the founding and settlement of the greater Saint Wendel area in Indiana. In fact, wealthy Wendel also donated land for the St. Wendel Catholic Church, named after his patron Saint and not himself, as well as the greater area of St. Wendel. Wendelen and Katharina's children were Marcus, Peter, Katherine, and Veronica.

Subsequently, son John M. Müller married Helena Dudenhoeffer, who was born on April 16, 1837 in Cincinnati, Ohio. Incidentally, the farmhouse described in this book was built in the year 1860 by John M. Müller, who was the Author's Grandfather.

The only child of John M. and Helena was John Herman Müller, born March 12, 1856, in Saint Wendel, Indiana. John Herman Müller married Mary Schmitt, who was born on October 25, 1858, in Princeton, Indiana. Their children were as follows:

- Joseph Francis Miller, born December 29, 1878. Joseph passed away on January 11, 1956, in Warren, Michigan, having turned 77 just 13 days earlier. He never married.
- Mary Barbara Miller, born January 2, 1881. Mary was a member of the Sisters of St. Francis in Oldenburg, Indiana, for over 16 years, having joined in 1907. She passed away on June 21, 1923, at the age of 42.
- Aloysius Miller, born January 21, 1883. Aloysius passed away of diphtheria on October 11, 1885, at the young age of two years and eight months.
- Francis "Frank" Sylvester Miller, born December 30, 1884. He was married to Dorothy Miller, which was her actual maiden name, though some records show his wife to be Rose Reising. Frank died on November 21, 1968, one month before his 84th birthday.
- Adam Miller, born Monday, May 30, 1887. Adam passed away from whooping cough on Friday, August 9, 1889, at the young age of two years and (not quite) three months. He died just one week before the birth of the next Miller child.
- John Aloysius Miller, the Author of this book. John was born on August 16, 1889. He passed on March 22, 1982
- Rose Marie Miller, born October 18, 1891. She passed away in March of 1969 in Warren, Michigan. Rose never married.
- Cecilia Anna Miller, born November 22, 1894. Cecilia married William John Tenbarge and had at least five children. She passed away on New Year's Eve, December 31, 1981, in Evansville, Indiana, at the age of 87.
- Helen Josephine Miller, born December 7, 1896. Helen married Walter LeMerise and had three children. She died in August of 1969 in Warren, Michigan.
- Henry Mark Miller, born January 16, 1900. He was the first Miller ancestor born in the 1900's. He was married to Teresa Miller and had four children. Henry passed away on January 7, 1973, just nine days short of his 73rd birthday.
- Clements Adam Miller, born Saturday, July 19, 1902. Clements died of pneumonia on Tuesday, February 17, 1903, at the age of seven months.

PHOTO SECTION

Wendelin and Katharina (Müller) Waszmer.
Katharina traveled to America from Darmstadt, Germany in 1832
with her parents, Nicklous and Katherena, and brother, John M.

The Author's parents, John Herman Müller and Mary Schmitt. It was John's father, John M. Müller, who built the farmhouse below.

The Müller Family posing at the farmhouse in the Spring of 1897.

Left to right:

- *Joseph (back) age 19.*
- *Francis "Frank" (in front of Joseph) age 13.*
- *Mother - Mary (sitting) age 39.*
- *Mary is holding baby Helen, age 4 months.*
- *Rose, age 6, standing between her parents.*
- *Father - John Herman (sitting) age 41.*
- *John is holding Cecilia, age 3.*
- *Mary (back right) age 19.*
- *John Aloysius, the author of this book, age 7 years, 8 months.*

A slightly wider photo of the Müller farmhouse. (Below) A photo of the property as it looks today, at the southwest intersection of Blake Road and Schmitt Road, 2.5 miles east of Wadesville, Indiana.

—The Mellus Newspapers' Photo

A PEEK INTO THE PAST — John Miller, of Lincoln Park, takes Mrs. Miller and two of their grandsons, John Shinavier (second from right) and Kenny Miller on an adventure into the past as he points out features of a scale model of his childhood home in Indiana. Miller spent some 500 hours in construction of the exact replica, which sets on an eight by eight foot base in the Millers' basement recreation room.

BLUEPRINT IS MEMORY 63 YEARS OLD

Parker Recreates Ancestral Home

An article from the local Lincoln Park, Michigan newspaper, dated December 6, 1959. The extended article, written by staff writer Mary C. Finley, describes the Author's recreation of his childhood home and farm. It read as follows:

"The elephant got his reputation for a remarkable memory from people who weren't aware of the memory-storing ability of small boys.

A 70-year-old Lincoln Park man, drawing on memories deposited in a secret vault of his brain in the first [13] years of his life, has just completed a scale model of the buildings on his ancestral farm in Indiana as they looked in 1896 – even to the placement of milk pails and butter crocks on a backyard shelf.

John Miller, of 1390 Warwick, estimates that he has spent about 500 hours of work on the project since he started the eight-square-foot layout in July [1959]. He used a scale of one-half inch to a foot.

The prototype for Miller's Lilliputian homestead was a 120-acre farm, near Evansville [Indiana], which had been in the Miller family for more than a half-century at the time of his birth. His great-grandfather, a plasterer who immigrated to Wheeling, West Virginia from Germany in 1832, moved by barge up the Ohio River to Evansville to purchase the farm in 1834 and [with his son, John M.] to build the two-story, six room house, each room with an inside measurement of 16 by 16 feet.

TWO KITCHENS. Extending back from the living area of the house were a one-story kitchen and summer kitchen. The front entrance to the house was a small portico, which the family called a "perdigo". Other farm buildings included a log barn, a log stable, a combination granary and tool shed, chicken houses, a hog house, a smoke house, and an outhouse. Using wood from packing cases discarded by area business concerns, Miller sawed each miniature plank to its proper scale for the buildings. The most intriguing feature of the layout, however, is its wealth of the small details which mark the difference between a house and a home.

CAREFUL WORK. Eaves troughs and gutter spouts, made in exact proportion to the house, were devised from tin cans. The lightning rods, so necessary to the farmhouse at the turn of the century, are reduced to gossamer wires for protection of the 17-by-27-inch model house. The familiar iron dinner bell, scaled to thimble size, hangs ready to summon an elfin family from the fields. Lights, shining through the windows, reveal green window shades and lace curtains. Two large cedar tress which fronted the house have shrunken to house plant size, and plum, cherry and peach trees stand in their original places around the yard.

FENCE TYPES. Miller was meticulous in his reproduction of fences. The yard was surrounded with white pickets, nailed to boards; pickets, woven with wire, enclosed the garden and truck crop plat; plank fences were used around the barnyard, and for the fields, oak rails, riven by Miller's great-grandfather, were crisscrossed along boundary lines. Firewood was an important part of life to farm people in Miller's youth, and cords of wood are stacked neatly along the plank fence of the barnyard – matchstick size pieces for a doll-sized kitchen range and larger sticks for a heating stove.

LOTS OF ANIMALS. The barnyard is not deserted either. Horses and colts, cows and calves, and hogs and piglets browse around the barn lot for food, and chickens, ducks and geese search for bugs and worms in the chicken yard. A small boy (Miller, perhaps) moves about the barnyard with a pail. Adding realism to the scene are two wagons, once with a hayrack and one fitted with a box-bed and seat; a rain barrel, which caught water for the family laundry; a "schnitzelbank", a type of homemade vise for holding wood; a grindstone and a stepstone with a hole in the center of each end. These holes were used as pestles by the children to crush soft bricks into dust for their mother's use as scouring powder.

BACKWARD GLIMPSE. *"Why did I make it?"* Miller, who has been a Lincoln Park resident for the past 30 years, smiled. *"Perhaps it was to give my grandchildren a glimpse of an age that has passed – an era when nobody had much money, but everybody who was willing to work had a good life."* Miller has brought some of his ancestors' ingenuity with him into the atomic age. His workshop, where he fashioned the intricate farm replica, is filled with homemade power tools. He shaped the wooden framework and his saws, sanders, lathe and drill and installed the proper wiring to operate them. Since his retirement a year ago from the Detroit Fruit Terminal, Miller has kept a stream of interesting objects rolling from his workshop. He has made a glass-fronted corner cupboard in which Mrs. Miller displays her bone china cups and saucers and other pretties.

MAKES TOYS. In a basement playroom for visiting grandchildren, doll beds, wooden trains, boats, trucks and cars await the clatter of small feet down the stairs. Shadow boxes, to be given as gifts, are his current project. Everything which comes from his workshop is made from scrap limber – a fact one would never guess from the finished pieces. Of all his creations, however, Miller finds the greatest satisfaction in the replica of his boyhood home. He finds it hard to understand that a visitor should be surprised at his memory of the farm and its buildings after a lapse of 63 years. *"My memory always has been keen and as for details, they are frequently more important than the big things. I was born in that house and I love it. Why shouldn't I remember the details? After all, I lived there [for 22] years."*

Present-day photos of the Müller family farm and homestead replica.

The original 1959 bulb used to light the house's interior still works.

(Below) The Editor (left) with brothers James and Peter (right).

(MORE) ABOUT THE AUTHOR

In February of 1912 at the age of 22, less than ten years after the timeline of this book ends, John Aloysius Miller left the Indiana family farm and moved to Detroit, Michigan. Following his arrival, he found work in the automotive environment, eventually settling and raising a family in the suburbs of Detroit.

In order to appreciate the period, it was two months after John left the Indiana farm that the RMS Titanic crashed into an iceberg in the northern Atlantic Ocean, sinking the ship within three hours of impact, and killing over 1,500 of the 2,224 passengers aboard.

Following his arrival in Detroit, John Miller found residence at 191 Dragoon Street, located between the I-75 Fisher Freeway and the Detroit River, just blocks from Historic Fort Wayne. There he rented a room from the Kramer family comprising of a grandfather, two daughters, and a nephew just out of high school.

John soon found work in the Studebaker Automotive Plant No. 3 located at Brush and Piquette Avenues. It was a 750,000 square foot facility that completed chassis for Special and Big Six models. He made good wages at Studebaker.

By Christmas the following year, John had met his future wife, Lucy Laura Lemerise. They were married on June 16, 1915, at the Holy Redeemer Catholic Church in Detroit, just one month after the sinking of the RMS Lusitania that subsequently pressured America to enter World War I.

John and Lucy Miller's children:

- Marcella Clara Miller, born April 17, 1916.
- Frances Marie Miller, born December 18, 1918.
- Bernadette Henrietta Miller, born November 3, 1920 (the Editor's mother).
- John Ernest (Jack) Miller, born September 1, 1925.
- James Remi Miller, born September 8, 1931.
- Gerald Joseph Miller, born October 7, 1933.

Lucy Lemerise-Miller passed on March 7, 1974, in their home in Lincoln Park, Michigan, following a fall down a portion of the second-floor stairs that resulted in the injury her of head. Husband John helped her to her bed where she subsequently passed. She was 79 years old. John Miller eventually moved to Spokane, Washington, to live with his daughter, Frances, and her husband, Leo. John Miller died on Monday, March 22, 1982, in Spokane, also as an end-result of falling down a flight of stairs. He was 92 years old.

ABOUT THE EDITOR

Christopher Locke is the Grandson of the book's Author, John Aloysius Miller, and his wife, Lucy Lemerise-Miller. Chris' mother, Bernadette, was John and Lucy's third child.

Chris grew up in Metro Detroit, and currently resides in SW Florida with his wife, Maggie.

You can reach Chris at CLocke426@aol.com.

Editor's Notes:

A very special thank you goes out to my cousin, Jennifer LeMerise Bickel, who inspired me to publish my Grandfather's book in this format. Jennifer's Grandmother was Helen Miller- LeMerise, my Grandfather's sister. Jennifer's Grandfather was Walter LeMerise, who happened to be a cousin of Lucy Lemerise Miller, my Grandmother.

Jennifer did an incredible job publishing my Grandfather's book on Blurb.com, which includes numerous photos, as well as a scan of each page of the original manuscript my Grandfather typed. The link to the book is as follows:

https://www.blurb.com/b/743902-memories-of-a-country-boy

Another thank you goes out to my brother, Peter Locke, for 'rescuing' the Müller family farm and homestead replica, built by our Grandfather.

My Grandfather had donated the entire scaled model set to the Lincoln Park Museum in Michigan before moving to Spokane, Washington. Unfortunately, Museum personnel was 'less than' considerate in its display and treatment of the set. Armed with written permission from our Grandfather, Pete confronted Museum personnel and removed the replica items from their storage room shelves.

As shown in previous photos, the complete scale model replica now rests in the basement of Peter's home in New Baltimore, Michigan, carefully preserved to the exact layout details as drawn by our Grandfather. The original 1959 lightbulb in the interior of the model house still works, and is only turned on for a few moments on Christmas Day.

Made in the USA
Columbia, SC
25 July 2020